Make Your Life
Extraordinary

Make Your Life
Extraordinary

Dr. Guy F. Riekeman

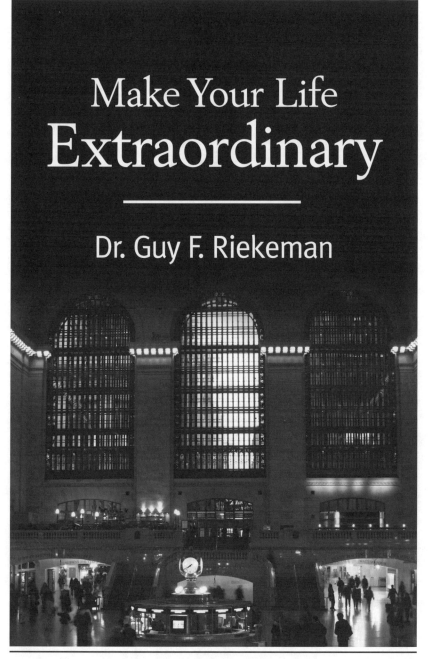

LIFE UNIVERSITY PRESS
2007

Life University Press
1005 Canyon Point Circle
Roswell, GA 30076

Library of Congress Control Number: 2007931991

ISBN 978-0-9763520-1-3

Manufactured in the United States of America

Edited by Randy Heuston
Designed by Ellen Glass

Dedication

This book is dedicated to my daughter Vanessa,
who took my hand at her birth and led me on
a 30-year journey of self-discovery that is still not complete.
She has grown into a beautiful, intelligent woman, wife and
mother. The Universe has let me be witness to her experiences,
growing pains and passions. Today she and her husband,
Dr. Jason Helfrich, practice chiropractic in Colorado Springs,
but she continues to provide me lessons
in personal awareness via my three grandsons,
who are mentioned frequently in this book:
Tyler, the chairman of my Intellectual Board of Trustees,
Caelen and Alex.

Contents

Acknowledgments

A special thanks to Letitia Sweitzer, who spent months researching 20 years of audio tapes of my lectures and found a way to capture the ideas and organize them coherently on paper. And then to my long-time friend Randy Heuston, a deep debt of gratitude laced with envy and admiration at his ability to cut to the core of the issue with a perfect quote or phrase or paragraph. Mixing his history as a newspaper man and our friendship, he was able to give my "voice" to the pages. And appreciation to Cynthia Boyd, D.C., who kept us on track and in communications with each other and the print world.

Life doesn't work when you attempt to do it by yourself, and mine doesn't work well without those who compensate for the areas of my life where there are "blind spots" in my brain. My best friends do more than go to movies with me or spend time taking walks around Manhattan or at my ranch in Colorado; they help me manage the most significant educational institution in redefining our current healthcare system, LIFE University in Atlanta Georgia. To Brian McAulay, Bill Jarr, Barry Nickelsberg, thanks for making work and dreaming and actualizing the future so much fun everyday. And kudos to my support staff, Nita Allen and Simone Branham. And to the two men who took me under their wings and taught how to lecture and administer a college, Dr. Joseph Flesia and Mike Crawford.

People often ask how long it took you to produce the book. A year of work, but really a lifetime of experiences. Actually, a couple of decades of being handled and pushed by people whose lives had been altered by the concepts and who endured more frustration than they should have in trying to get these ideas, stories and life models out of my lecture rooms around the world and into printed text. At the top of that list, Annie Schmitt, who never failed to remind me of my commitment to get it done. And to Barbara DeAngelis, Ph.D., who has authored numerous best sellers on relationships for taking the time to educate me on the process and offered her professional contacts along the way. And finally, to my dear friend Erica Peabody, D.C., who brought me to the "edge" and then enticed me to chance looking foolish by jumping and then jumped with me.

I spent my early professional career building a name for myself often on the road 45 weekends a year. At one point I burned out and dropped out and spent two and a half years on the beach in Santa Monica. Coming off that beach and going back into the "world" was the hardest thing I've ever had to do. I hope that at this point in my life I've gained some valuable insights about integrity being the most critical issue for each of us personally and for humanity at large. I strive every day to translate these lessons into tolerance, respect and meaningful relationships. I dream and build for a future where we can produce dialogue on the world's greatest conversations [thanks for that phrase, Bill O'Brien]. I apologize to those, especially my family, who, as Yeats wrote, were left screaming in the dark as I followed my passions and dreams. As Robin Williams said in *Dead Poets Society*, "The powerful play of life goes on and you may contribute a verse. What will your verse be?" I strive for the answer to that question every day. This book is a piece of that complex discovery. I hope you can use it and the other books that are coming to add distinction to your day-to-day experiences and thus make your life extraordinary.

Foreword

At the end of the movie *Castaway*, Tom Hanks' character literally stands at a crossroads, contemplating what to do with the rest of his life. While marooned he had tried suicide, then rejected the idea and carried out his plan to get off the island. Now, back in civilization, discovering that the woman he so dearly loves has become another man's wife, he carries a far deeper understanding of how both conscious decisions and random circumstance can alter one's life forever.

That motion picture provides us powerful images touching on the human condition, and one of the messages, of course, is the vital importance of taking responsibility for our actions. That is the mandate of philosophers like Ayn Rand and the Existentialists, and most of us, whatever our philosophical or religious leaning, would agree that taking responsibility for what we think and do is a prerequisite to finding meaning and satisfaction in our lives.

Popular shows also have dramatized the so-called "butterfly effect" of chaos theory. This holds that a slight change at the beginning of a process—like the flapping of the wings of an insect—can set in motion far-reaching changes. From *It's a Wonderful Life* to Ray Bradbury's *The Sound of Thunder* to the movie *Butterfly Effect* to episodes of the TV sitcom *Scrubs* and even *The Simpsons*, the media races our imagination with the notion that, if we could only enter a time machine and do something different way back when, things would be spectacularly different now.

However, the practical lesson here—indeed the moral impera-tive—is if we start doing the right things today we may really alter the future for the better, even if we don't live to see it. In other words, we ought to take responsibility for our actions not only for the sake of our own happiness but also for the sake of things greater than our-selves. Yes, we're talking about supplying real substance to the well-worn wish to "make a difference in the world."

This book—an updated version of lectures I have been giving and refining for many years—organizes these two concepts of our need to take individual responsibility and our power to make a difference around the theme *Make Your Life Extraordinary*. The book is pub-lished in conjunction with my current lecture tour, which is scheduled to hit 100 major cities during the course of about two years. Fittingly, it's called the "Power of One Tour," and it's delivering a values-laden message to thousands looking for further inspiration and increased determination to improve their lives and change the world.

Although my professional background is in the dynamically grow-ing profession of chiropractic, the people invited to the Power of One presentations are, for the most part, not chiropractors but chiropractic patients, their families and friends, high school and college students and faculty, civic and business leaders, and others from many back-grounds—in short, just ordinary people with a more-than-ordinary interest in improving the quality of their own lives and those lives they touch.

Since I have been talking about these themes for a long time, I know they resonate with people from many walks of life. Not only that, but I have come to know hundreds of people who actually began to act on my message and the good examples of others such as those mentioned in this book, people who took risks, made changes and experienced the added richness those changes brought.

Although this book incorporates much of the material of my lectures, it also pursues some aspects in depth not possible in a talk of a couple of hours. For example, I've added mini-profiles of five people who stand as shining examples of extraordinary lives. I've also sprinkled in quotations that suggest a context larger than my own thoughts because so much of what I've concluded in my own life, and want to share with you, I owe to many, many others. I am in their debt, and you will be as well.

That being said, this is also a very personal book. The people I feature are people I connect with at a profound level even though I haven't personally met them all. I would hope that you also would use this book as an incentive to look more closely at people you know or read about, those whose lives can bring you more courage, hope and passion for excellence. Find your own personal heroes, as I have, and you'll find deeper understanding of your own potential along the way.

Please accept this book with my personal best wishes that it will help you, too, find a path to make your life extraordinary.

Sincerely,

Dr. Guy F. Riekeman
January 1, 2007

Watch for these Five on Five

This book was prepared in conjunction with Dr. Guy Riekeman's "Power of One Tour," taking him to about 100 cities throughout North America. During his tour appearances, Dr. Riekeman highlights five ordinary people who do extraordinary things. All five also have five values in common. As you read through **Make Your Life Extraordinary,** watch for those five profiles, and see if you can figure out by the end of the book what those five values are that they hold in common.

MAKE YOUR LIFE EXT

ARE YOU READY TO STOP BEING A TOTAL ZERO?

CHAPTER   TITLE

1

:: GRAND CENTRAL STATION

:: LIVING AT ZERO

:: WAITING FOR "IT"

CREATE YOUR OWN LIFE

Everyone thinks
of changing the world,
but no one thinks
of changing himself.
LEO TOLSTOY

CHAPTER ONE

Are You Ready to Stop Being a Total Zero?

Is your life today the extraordinary one you wished for years ago?
Or are you just "beached"?

———

IN THESE DAYS WHEN INFORMATION CAN BE REROUTED IN A NANO-second over the Internet and a weather or terrorist alert can change the flight patterns of a hundred jumbo jets at once, we're very familiar with how quickly our thinking and entire lives can take a new direction. It wasn't always like this.

As we're often told, back in the day of our great-grandparents, grandparents and even our parents, change happened less often. Sure, there were dramatic shifts brought by the Industrial Revolution, two World Wars, and a myriad of inventions, but changes were fewer and the pace of change relatively slower. An advantage then, too, was that we believed we could clearly discern in hindsight what the changes were and what they had wrought.

Today we know things are changing in quantum leaps, but we so often feel powerless because we simply don't know what's driving us or what's causing the world to act so crazy. We realize change is all around us, but we have trouble keeping up with what the changes really are, let alone what they're doing to us.

So, I'd like to slow things down a bit and draw on a metaphor that has some history to it, in fact, has stuck rather than just passing through popular consciousness. This metaphor can help us understand not only how we're whipsawed by change but also how we can initiate change to our benefit.

Grand Central Station

Although relatively few people have been there, powerful images nevertheless spring to mind when we mention "Grand Central Station." The cavernous railway station in Manhattan has become synonymous with crowds and commotion, hustling and dodging, people intent on their own individual agendas scurrying toward their work or their homes, attaché case in one hand, raincoat or a Starbucks coffee cup in the other.

Those who have been to Grand Central Station know that its history is an exciting and complicated tapestry—the building has undergone repeated reconfigurations, barely escaped demolition and today stands in its historic splendor—and its architecture is grand, the huge windows like those of a cathedral, light streaming through in almost palpable columns onto the people hurrying for the trains below. It's as we might imagine God's communicating with Moses, Mohammed or Jesus.

When you stand in Grand Central Station, you feel overwhelmed with the magnitude and, yes, the majesty. You feel lost in the jostling crowd. It's like the seaman's prayer, "Oh Lord, your ocean's so big, and my boat is so small." You can't help but be humbled at Grand Central Station.

That's one reason I like this image as a metaphor. It communicates power and a more-than-ordinary importance to seemingly mundane events. It's reminiscent of Tom Hanks at the crossroads in

Castaway. Besides, we've all been jostled by crowds and felt the panic that we might miss the train or plane or board the wrong one. Grand Central is an image most of us can relate to better than bits and bytes over the Internet. And it summons up, I believe, a sense of urgency about where we're going with our lives.

Whether or not you've been in Grand Central Station when the trains are leaving the Big Apple at the evening rush hour, imagine yourself there now. Imagine hundreds of thousands of frazzled business people and service industry workers dumping out of the city on trains headed out to the suburbs.

Let's say I'm headed to White Plains, and in 15 minutes I have to get to Track A to catch my 7:21 train. As I head to my train, I bump into people headed for their own trains. We may knock each other off course, but, since we know where we're headed, we adjust our paths and keep going. I know I can't stop to buy a newspaper because I can't take the time to wait in line; I might miss my train. While I'm making my way to the train on Track A leaving at 7:21, I hear the announcer on the public address system (although the voice is somewhat indistinct amid the hubbub) say the White Plains train has been delayed; it is now scheduled to leave at eight o'clock from Track C. I stop. Reorient. I have time to buy a newspaper.

Later I head to Track C. I bump into someone else. But now, because I've stopped and changed my direction, everything in Grand Central Station is altered. I don't bump into the people I would have bumped into trying to get to the 7:21 train. They move ahead of me while I go over to buy a newspaper. They bump into someone else instead.

What difference do these small changes make, you may wonder. Who knows? I do know that people get different seats on the train than they would have gotten without the schedule change. Who knows but what two strangers may sit beside each other as a result, and in about a year they'll get married? Who knows who decides to have dinner instead of waiting for the eight o'clock train and ends up taking the nine o'clock train instead? And maybe the taxi that meets the nine o'clock train has an accident taking that person home. And that person has surgery to repair his injuries, followed by chiropractic care and because of that care decides to study chiropractic. Who knows? But we do know things change. And we do know of things in our own lives that have happened to us by chance meetings and missed trains or flights. In other words, the decisions we make day to day, yes, even second to second, literally alter not only our lives in somewhat meaningful ways but also the lives of all the people with whom we engage.

I am suggesting to you that how we show up at Grand Central Station, wherever we are headed, whom we bump into, the relationships that we create in the course of our lifetime, what we do in the course of the day, moment to moment, has an impact on the structure of the universe and on people as a whole. This concept has been popularized in the so-called "butterfly effect," a facet of chaos theory that postulates that a small change early in a sequence or process can determine dramatic changes down the line. My premise is that, if we want the impact of our lives to be positive for the future of humanity, we have to live each moment to its maximum degree of excellence.

Living at Zero

When we head into Grand Central Station, carrying our baggage, looking neither to the left or the right, we arrive as a zero, most of us. We arrive as ordinary. We have intent—to catch a certain train—but

6

we don't have awareness or vision or commitment. We exhibit no power or leadership. We have our baggage, and we have our blinders on. We are ordinary. Zero.

Most of the world has accepted that mediocrity is all right, that mediocrity is enough. Ayn Rand, one of the great philosophers of our time, said, "Most people are satisfied living their lives at zero." What she meant was that living at zero means not having the best career or business possible, just as long as you can get by. Living at zero means not being as healthy as you can be as long as you don't have any pain. See, that's what most people do with regard to their health. They don't come to their doctor to be extraordinarily healthy. They come in just to get by without pain.

You have to expect things of yourself before you can do them.
MICHAEL JORDAN

Living at zero means not being as successful as you can be financially, just as long as you don't have bill collectors calling you at all hours or a repo man in your driveway. Living at zero means not having the best marriage relationship that you have the ability to create; you just don't have to go through a messy divorce.

Most of the world has accepted that it's okay to survive at zero. I contend that the real joys in life lie beyond zero. They're in an area that we call "living our lives extraordinarily." It's not necessarily a matter of degree. You're either living extraordinarily or you're not. It's like being pregnant. Either you are or you aren't.

What most of us are doing is either living extraordinarily, a handful of us, or we're what I call "beached." That happened to me. I was one of those workaholics. I thought that the harder you work the better things should get, and that, if you could accomplish all of your goals—get the big salaries and the prestigious promotions and the mahogany desk—that would make you happy. And I got all mine. One day I woke up and realized that I had it all. It was the most miserable moment of my life.

I'm reminded of Peggy Lee's great rendition of the song, "Is That All There Is?" The chorus goes:

Is that all there is, is that all there is?
If that's all there is, my friends, then let's keep dancing.
Let's break out the booze and have a ball.
If that's all there is. . . .

So I quit and dropped out. At least I had the guts to stop doing what I was doing. I went and lay on a beach in southern California for two and a half years. I had enough money stashed away that I could do that. And, by the way, when people tell you that you'd get tired of that after a while, it's a lie. It was wonderful, if self-indulgence is what you crave. Beach time is all right for a couple weeks of replenishing self-care. But two years is an escape from responsibility. It's not living your life extraordinarily.

Most people are beached because they're not living extraordinarily. Your beach may mean that you come home every day after not enjoying your work and you plop down in front of the television so you don't have to deal with anything or anybody. Then, during the course of the evening, you stuff some food in your mouth to get a little enjoyment. You watch TV until late at night. After Leno or Letterman is over, you turn off the television and stagger into bed (your family went there hours before). You wake up groggy the next morning, get out of bed, slop more food in your face, head off to work that you're not going to enjoy, and you're going to do that for the next 20, 40, 60 years of your life. I call that being beached, only you're not getting the tan.

On the other hand, babies live at 100 per cent. You can't stop them. They sleep at 100 percent. You can be carrying a sleeping baby lying up against your shoulder and you can walk through a department store or Grand Central Station and, if they want to sleep, they sleep. When they wake up and want to explore, they explore. When they see a toy on a shelf or a cookie in your hand, or a fragile glass figurine on the table, they go for it. I know a toddler, barely walking, who, when he hears the dishwasher being opened in the kitchen, makes a beeline for it. He's wobbling and even though he may fall over, he's going 100 percent to get into those forks and spoons in the little rack. You can't stop a baby from going for what he wants at 100 per cent.

It's when they become adolescents—that means becoming near-adult, although it seems like a misnomer sometimes—that you see signs of being beached.

Waiting for "It"

I remember when my daughter, Vanessa, turned 13. I was tucking her into bed after her birthday party, and I said to her, "Ness, how does it feel to be a teen-ager?" I wouldn't want to go back to 13 from this direction and do that one over again, but coming at it from the other direction should be aces, shouldn't it? Hitting 13 is a time in your life when you say, "My life's going to be different now. I'm different from when I was 12," even though it's just been 24 hours. And it is different because we say so, isn't it? Jewish kids have their bar mitzvahs when they turn 13 for good reason.

And so I was tucking her in that night saying, "Ness, how does it feel to be 13, to be a teen-ager?" And her response was, "Dad, just three more years!" Three more years meant what? Being 16 and getting a driver's license. And at 13, she knew that on her 16th birthday her life would be transformed forever. It's all she talked about for the next two and a half years. She even got a car. During her summers, instead of being in California where our family hangs out for the summer or in Europe where we travel, she spent her whole school vacation in Colorado Springs, slopping yogurt for minimum wage just to raise enough money so she could buy a car. She got a VW Cabriolet that sat in the garage because she couldn't even drive yet. She went out and polished it daily, and she knew that her life was about to be transformed because of the car on the day she turned 16.

Don't wait for the last judgment. It takes place every day.

ALBERT CAMUS

What I knew and she didn't yet know was that she'd get her driver's license and there would be 48, maybe 72, hours of joy and excitement before the agenda would kick in. What she didn't realize was that she was now going to be the taxi driver of the family. Instead of me running her sister around to gymnastics meets and dropping her off at school early in the morning and picking her up afterwards, Vanessa was given an agenda for her days, a more adult agenda than she'd had before. And then, of course, there were the insurance and repairs and lube jobs and fixing tires. All of a sudden, she realized that, gosh, getting a car wasn't "it." It wasn't the transformation she'd expected.

It's not bad that Vanessa was excited about getting a car. It would have been a shame if she weren't. It would be a shame if she didn't get joy as the reward for all those hours dipping yogurt. What's bad about it was that she thought getting a car is "it," that it was what life was all about. She'd been waiting for "it" to happen to her for 15 and a half years.

But don't feel bad for her. She was an adolescent. Feel bad that most people in their 40s and 50s are also waiting for "it" to happen to them. They believe that, if they can just get the right house, the right car, the right marriage, the right practice or job, the right number of new clients or customers that, gosh, then maybe "it" could really happen to them. They don't even know what "it" is, but they think it hasn't happened to them yet.

Vanessa got her driver's license, and that wasn't "it." Was getting a license "it" for you? Is that what transformed your life and made it worthwhile being here on this earth? No. And then she decided turning 18 and graduating from high school must be "it." You get to go out and live on your own, and you don't have to go to all of those stupid high school classes any longer. When she was 18 and a high school graduate, she got to go to college where she found you have to spend all of your time, not in a stupid class, but a stupid library doing your own work because there's more responsibility then. What's more, living on your own isn't all it's trumped up to be. When you're living on your own, there are no more shopping sprees with your mom and dad. All of a sudden there are no more great houses. Now, you're living on a couple hundred bucks a month with eight other people in a three-bedroom house, sharing it with the rats and roaches, aren't you? So, you know what? Going off to college isn't "it."

Then, it's, gosh, maybe when I get out of college, get a great job, then I can live by myself and get the house I really want. Maybe that's "it." Then, it could be a relationship. Maybe that's "it." Then, maybe it's having kids because the relationship wasn't "it." Then, maybe it's going to college or graduate school so you can really make some bucks. Maybe that's "it." Then, maybe it's doubling your professional practice or doubling your sales. You know what, you could wait your whole life for "it" to happen to you and die in your bed never having been alive one moment of the entire time you're here. That's the scary part.

If you've been waiting for "it" to happen to you, let me tell you something: *This* is "it." It's not getting any better than this, and it's not getting any worse than this; this is "it." Until you come to that realization, you can't really make your life extraordinary.

Here's a quote I like: "For a long time, it had seemed to me that my life was about to begin, real life that is. But there was always some obstacle in the way, something to be got through first. Some unfinished business, time still to be served, debt to be paid, then life could begin. At last, it dawned on me that these obstacles were my life."

Create Your Own Life

By being born, you weren't guaranteed the right to live extraordinarily. What you were given was the possibility of creating your life the way you wanted to create it and that's what we're talking about because most of us, while we were given the possibility of creating the life that we want, never seized on that possibility. When we were born, our goal was to survive in a world of circumstances we didn't choose. When we were growing up, we had to learn how to survive in the sandbox with our siblings and friends, and then we had to learn how to survive the first day we went to school. Then, we had to learn how to survive when we got our driving license, went to college, got a job to pay the bills, or got a divorce. Our whole life has been about how to survive, and very few people ever say, "Hold it! Where do I get this life from?" And, since they never ask the question, they never come to the realization that their life was not something they created; it was something that was created *for* them. It was created *for* them by their parents, their schoolteachers, their environment, television and their religious leaders, and never once did we sit down and say, "Is this the life that I would have created if I could have created it from scratch?"

An even better question, the question we are about to deal with in this book, is this: "Is this the life I would create if I could create it on a moment-to-moment basis starting right now?" I contend that most of us would have created it differently if we had to do the creating. I'm telling you now that you have the possibility to recreate your life and make it extraordinary. The only other option is mere survival, the thing we've been raised with, just getting by in relationships, in our jobs and with our children. Mere survival.

There's a fine line between fishing and just standing on the shore like an idiot.

STEPHEN WRIGHT

Most people spend their entire life looking good, or at least trying to. Do you know how hard— and expensive—it is to always look good? Even if you're beached—especially if you're beached—you're holding your stomach in, trying to look good. I contend that if you're spending your whole life trying to look good, you don't have the opportunity of creating the life that you want.

So, we're going to consider how to recreate our lives, how to make our lives extraordinary. To live an extraordinary life, you have to live your life at 100 percent—as you did when you were a toddler before you began to wait for "it." Only now you have some chance of knowing what ideal, cause, career or relationship deserves your hundred percent. And you know what you're looking for: A change you can make that will take your life from zero to extraordinary.

POINTS TO PONDER

- Things are changing all around us. The good news is that, as we take responsibility to initiate some of those changes ourselves, we can make an impact on the world.

- Most people live the lives that were handed to them by others or by circumstances. That's living at zero. You, though, can create the life you want if you are willing to really go for it. You can make your life extraordinary.

- Don't live your life in expectation of one supposedly magical "it" to make you happy; instead, create your life every waking moment by showing up for everything with a commitment to excellence.

PROFILE

Vaclav Havel

HIS PEN WAS 'MIGHTIER THAN THE SWORD'

Vaclav Havel's life illustrates the power of words and ideas to change the world. His insightful plays and essays assaulted the rationale of Czechoslovakian communism by laying bare its moral bankruptcy, appealing to the higher good in individuals and Czech society.

Born to a middle-class family in Prague, the future playwright, political dissident and president of his country, worked at various odd jobs while pursuing his studies. After serving two years in the military, he became a stage hand at a Prague theater while studying stagecraft. During the early 1960s, Havel wrote his first plays, ridiculing the Czechoslovakian police state. During the 1960s, Havel became an activist, criticizing government censorship at a writers congress in 1967; he became chairman of the Independent Writers Union the following year. Following the suppression of the Prague Spring in 1968, he was banned from the theatre and became even more politically active, culminating with the publication of the Charter 77 manifesto. His political activities resulted in multiple stays in prison, the longest being four years, and he was subjected to constant government harassment. Already a well-known playwright in the West, during the 1980s Havel also gained widespread recognition as a dissident, receiving the

Dutch Erasmus Prize in 1986. In 1989, he helped found Civic Forum, the first legal opposition movement in his country since the late 1940s. Later that year, after the "Velvet Revolution" had deposed the communist dictatorship, Havel was chosen president of Czechoslovakia. In spite of some serious health problems, he kept this position through the breakup of the Czech Republic and Slovakia, and has guided the Czech Republic through a successful transition to a liberal, free-market system and NATO membership. Havel's writings had an enormous impact on the dismantling of the totalitarian regime in Czechoslovakia. He noted: "I really do inhabit a system in which words are capable of shaking the entire structure of government, where words can prove mightier than ten military divisions. . . ."

MAKE YOUR LIFE EXT...

CHAPTER   TITLE

**2   AN EXCITING LIFE
MAY BE ONLY AN INCH AWAY**

:: DECIDING TO REALLY LIVE

:: THAT EXTRA INCH

*The moment one
definitely commits oneself,
then providence moves too. . . .
Whatever you can do or dream you can,
begin it. Boldness has genius, power
and magic in it. Begin it now.*

JOHANN WOLFGANG GOETHE

CHAPTER TWO

An Exciting Life May Be Only an Inch Away

To this point maybe you haven't created your life.
To start creating it now will take fresh thinking and extra effort.

WHEN I WAS HANGING OUT ON THE BEACH FOR TWO AND a half years, I had one breakthrough. I realized that 80 years from now nobody is going to care that you or I were ever here. Do you also think about that? In fact, to be honest with you, there aren't a whole lot of people who care right now, are there? If we all cashed it in today, for whatever reason, in the next few days there would be some wailing and gnashing of teeth for about an hour, and then all of those people at your funeral are going to go back to work the next day. That's just the way it is. Not too many people really care.

One of the most gut-wrenching poems I ever read was "Out, Out—" by Robert Frost. You may recall it is the story of a boy cutting wood with a chainsaw, the serene Vermont mountains in the background. When his sister calls him for supper, the chain saw slips and cuts deep into his hand:

Since he was old enough to know, big boy
Doing a man's work, though a child at heart—

He saw all spoiled. "Don't let him cut my hand off—
The doctor, when he comes. Don't let him, sister!"
So. But the hand was gone already.
The doctor put him in the dark of ether.
He lay and puffed his lips out with his breath.
And then—the watcher at his pulse took fright.
No one believed. They listened at his heart.
Little-less-nothing!—and that ended it.
No more to build on there. And they, since they
Were not the one dead, turned to their affairs.

With the mountains off in the distance, Frost gives us the sense of the silent and eternal universe, unmoved by the affairs of men. In his description of the boy, working as a man but envisioning all life ahead of him, the poet captures the essence of the potential we might fulfill. Then, with the tragic accident, he reminds us how quickly all can be spoiled, how futile life can be, especially when cut short. And finally, "They, since they were not the one dead, turned to their affairs." It's not that people are always calloused or cruel; it's just that we are limited in what we can do for each other, and certainly we cannot bring our loved ones back from the dead.

Living at risk is jumping off the cliff and building your wings on the way down.

RAY BRADBURY

To me this poem adds urgency to our deciding to make wise decisions about ourselves, our families, our friends and our possible impact on the world. That includes taking the proper precautions—the chain saw went out of control perhaps only by an inch—with a view to fulfilling our life's potential before it ends whenever that may be.

Deciding to Really Live

Walker Percy in *The Last Self-Help Book* tells the difference between a man who never considers committing suicide, which Percy calls the logical solution to depression, and a man who almost commits suicide. The man who realizes he has the option to keep on living or to die—like Hamlet in his "To be or not to be" speech—this man puts the gun to his head and considers whether to pull the trigger. He can go either way. When he chooses to put the gun away, when he chooses to live, he's not just accepting what life hands him, he's taking life into his own hands. "Since he has the option of being dead, he has nothing to lose by being alive. It is good to be alive," Percy says, adding that the man who made the choice to live can laugh and go to work "because he knows he doesn't have to." He has an option.

The famous Russian novelist Fyodor Dostoyevsky once stood before a firing squad, waiting for death, before a reprieve came at the last moment. He and the others lined up to be shot reacted to their brush with death in various ways. One of them lost his sanity. But for Dostoyevsky, the firing squad experience gave him a new appreciation for life, even though he was headed for prison. Here's what he wrote to his brother:

> *Life is a gift, life is happiness, every minute will be an eternity of happiness! Si jeunesse savait! [If youth only knew!]. . . . My brother, I do not feel despondent and have not lost heart. Life is life everywhere. Life is in ourselves and not outside us. There will be men beside me [in prison], and the important thing is to be a man among men and to remain a man always, whatever the misfortunes, not to despair and not to fall—that*

*is the aim of life, that is its purpose. I realize this now. The
idea has entered into my flesh and my blood. Yes, that is the
truth!...I have still got my heart and the same flesh and
blood which can love and suffer and pity and remember, and
that is also life. Never before have I felt such abundant and
healthy reserves of spiritual life in me as now....*
[Joseph Frank, The Years of Ordeal *(Princeton: Princeton
University Press, 1990) 62-63. Quoted from Dostoevsky's*
Pisma, I: 129 – 131.*]*

In a sense, until you get to that moment in your life and then
choose to be alive, you can't ever be fully alive. And until like Dostoyevsky you really understand that life, whatever its sorrows, is too
wonderful to waste, you haven't chosen life; you've just accepted it.

Now, I'm not telling you to walk out at your lunch break and
think about pulling the trigger or put yourself in front of a firing
squad. I'm saying that, until you've come to the realization that
whether you're here or not doesn't matter much to anyone else, you
can't create the life you want and you can't live fully. Until you
choose to be truly alive for yourself, then the only thing you have left
is what you've probably done your whole life, which is just to survive
in the face of the circumstances that have confronted you. What
we're doing in this book is considering how to create your life or
maybe *recreate* it in the way you want it to be.

We need to find out *how* to create the circumstances that we
want. Vaclav Havel did that in Czechoslovakia. A playwright and professor, Havel didn't try to figure out how to just get by in the face of
the Communist regime under which he lived. Because he couldn't
find the circumstances he wanted, he set about to create them. He

wrote protests and circulated petitions challenging civil rights abuses by Communist leaders and was jailed several times for his civil rights activities. This college professor was a key figure in the movement that brought communism down. In 1989, he was elected interim president of Czechoslovakia and promised to bring free elections for a permanent president. He served two five-year terms in this new democratic system. And he said something like this in his presentation to the United States Congress in the summer of 2003: "Don't ever use our names, the people in our movement, in the same sentences with words like 'heroes' and 'pioneers' because we weren't and we aren't. We were just a group of people that finally got to a point in our lives where it didn't matter any longer."

It's life, Jim ... but not as we know it.

MR. SPOCK

Isn't it intriguing that in order to create the thing we want, we have to get to the point where "it" doesn't matter any longer? Isn't it funny that relationships, before they can get really good sometimes, have to get to a point where there's nothing left to lose in them? So, you get to create them over again. While it's more dramatically apparent that you *must choose* to fully live if you face the possibility of death and you choose life, with a little imagination you can make that same choice from the beach or from the safety of your living room. You can choose to live at 100 percent. You can choose to live an extraordinary life. You can choose it today.

That Extra Inch

Some years ago, I participated in a workshop up in the mountains. One event was a "ropes course," which, you probably know, involves going into the mountains to do extraordinary things with ropes. We encountered a "zip line," which is a 500-foot line that is suspended from the top of the mountain and runs at about a 30-degree angle down to the ground. We walked out from the edge of a cliff on a board that was so narrow that the sides of our feet were hanging over the edges. This board was cantilevered about six feet out from the edge of this cliff.

Of course, we were all hooked up with safety equipment. We weren't doing stupid things out here, but even so, when you walk out over the edge of a 250-foot cliff, you're not totally unconcerned just because you know you're hooked up to safety equipment.

Running along this zip line was a set of wheels with a little handlebar. You walk out to the edge of the platform, hang your toes over the edge of the board, reach over your head, grab the handlebar attached to the wheels, and then they tell you, "Lean forward." And, as you lean forward, you get almost to the point of no return where your center of gravity is about to take you off the edge of the board. You hang there for as long as you can. Then they tell you, "Now, lean just a little more forward."

Men do change, and change comes like a little wind that ruffles the curtains at dawn, and it comes like the stealthy perfume of wildflowers hidden in the grass.

JOHN STEINBECK

The logical part of you knows you're not going to die, but another part of you feels as if your life hangs in the balance at that moment. You have to choose between the possibility of living life to the fullest—living at 100 percent—and the certainty of living life as you always have, staying in your comfort zone no matter how ordinary.

Most people, at some point in their life, get out to the edge of that board and they lean a little bit, and all it would take for them to have an extraordinary experience is one more inch. And they hold back from the inch. It's easy to walk the six feet out there. It's hard to just do the last inch. They cling to the board with their toes and hold their breath, trying to pull back from the abyss. Anyway, in this ropes course, there was no way back. They don't let you come back from this board. So, when you get out there, they say, "Now, lean forward. Now, lean a little more forward." And, finally, you lean far enough forward that you can't recover and, all of a sudden, you're moving 35 miles an hour, just hanging onto a handlebar down this 500-foot line.

The people who design these events figure, if you can jump off a 250-foot cliff, you probably can go back and appear on stage, or take out a loan and start a business, or tell your spouse, "Honey, I was wrong to do what I did, and I'm sorry." Because you have jumped, you know you can do more than what you have been doing; you can be bolder than you've been in the past. I contend that, if you walked into your office every day and lived your life at 100 percent and your relationships at 100 percent, magical things would happen.

What is the difference between professionals earning, say, $50,000 a year versus their earning $200,000 a year? Is it paperwork, procedures, hours, the appearance of the waiting room? No. I'm telling you, the difference lies in whether they've committed themselves to an extraordinary life, whether they're living at 100 percent. Similarly, the difference between a great relationship and a not-so-great relationship is probably about one inch. Are you going to lean a little bit forward? Are you going to take the handle and hang on as you ride into an extraordinary life?

I recently discovered the book and video entitled *212° The Extra Degree*. It's a motivational message about how extra effort makes all the difference. One degree above 211 causes water to boil. That turns water to steam, which can power a locomotive. Applied to human affairs, as the video powerfully conveys, the margin of victory—and the degree of reward—are often the result of a very slight difference. For instance, in Indy 500 races over 10 years, the average difference between first and second was 1.54 seconds. The winner took home an average of $1,278,813 while second place took home $621,321. The message of *212° The Extra Degree* is: "It's your life. You are responsible for the results. It's time to turn up the heat."

Yes, it's time to lean the extra inch. Time to put forth the extra degree of effort. Just as carelessness or inattention or a wrong decision—like the chain saw out of control by an inch—can change our lives for the worse or even end them altogether, so, too, sharper focus, right decisions and a little more effort can produce extraordinary rewards.

Are you ready to lean forward the extra inch? Are you ready to turn up the heat?

MEDITATE ON THIS

- You must come to the profound existential realization that life is short and precious, and that you can do more than just get by; you ought to take advantage of all life has to offer.

- An inch may mean the difference between disaster and success. Pay attention to both threats and opportunities, and act with both energy and wisdom.

- You don't have to accept the life you were handed by others or by circumstances. Make up your mind you can create the life you want with just an extra degree of effort and willingness to take a risk.

*If I had influence with
the good fairy who is supposed
to preside over the christening of all
children, I should ask that her gift to
each child in the world be a sense of
wonder so indestructible that it
would last throughout life.*

RACHEL CARSON

CHAPTER THREE

Are You *Really Aware* of...?

All powerful movements start with awareness.
If you are serious about moving to an extraordinary life, look
around, no, really look around . . . and beneath . . . and through.

―――――――

Y
OU'VE DECIDED, I HOPE, TO LEAN FORWARD AN INCH, THE
inch that stands between your ordinary life and an extraordinary life. You've decided to add that one degree of effort in
order to live at 100 percent. If so, you're in for an exciting ride.

What do you need to create this new life? There's integrity and
leadership and other qualities that motivational speakers often talk
about, and you'll read about later, but first there's something less
obvious but absolutely essential. *Awareness.*

You can't change your life or change the world without being
aware of what needs changing, and you don't know what needs
changing until you are aware of *what is.*

Let's begin with sensory awareness. Do we react to sights and
sounds, and let those reactions touch us mentally and emotionally?
Leonardo Da Vinci believed that knowledge and truth begins with
the senses, but that sadly the average human "looks without seeing,
listens without hearing, touches without feeling, eats without tasting,
moves without physical awareness, inhales without awareness of
odour or fragrance, and talks without thinking." Da Vinci would say

that, until we become aware with our senses, we can't think or act above mediocrity.

The Japanese poetic form *haiku* is perhaps the purest literary expression of that sort of awareness. Here's a famous one by Basho:

On a bare branch
a crow settles,
autumn dusk.

The writer observes a crow settling on a branch the way dusk settles in autumn, and evidently finds a metaphor for old age and approaching death. The viewer, perhaps the poet himself, is like a bare branch, stripped of the freshness and fruitage of youth. The dark, foreboding crow is a harbinger of death. Autumn, though, is simply a changing season, and the viewer sees himself undramatically slipping into the lifeless night.

> *We must learn to reawaken and keep ourselves awake, not by mechanical aid, but by an infinite expectation of the dawn.*
>
> HENRY DAVID THOREAU

So the Japanese poet is keenly tuned in to what he sees, hears, smells and feels. His awareness of nature translates into an awareness of his own life and death. A quiet, solitary epiphany.

In contrast, Vaclav Havel expressed his awareness regarding politics and governmental systems. Havel was not just another anti-Communist protester. He had an awareness of societal and economic conditions that bred communism, but he understood that those conditions reflected something deeper, a profound change in values brought about by society's enthronement of science and rationalism in place of the natural and the spiritual. In his influential essay "Politics and

Conscience," he recalls walking to school as a boy and seeing a factory's belching smokestack "soiling the heavens." His awareness went beyond environmental concern—after all, a scrubber could clean up that and other smokestacks. Rather, Havel saw matters this way:

> The chimney "soiling the heavens" is not just a technologically corrigible flaw of design, or a tax paid for a better consumerist tomorrow, but a symbol of a civilization which has renounced the absolute, which ignores the natural world and disdains its imperatives. So, too, the totalitarian systems warn of something far more serious than Western rationalism is willing to admit. They are, most of all, a convex mirror of the inevitable consequences of rationalism, a grotesquely magnified image of its own deep tendencies, an extreme offshoot of its own development and an ominous product of its own expansion. They are a deeply informative reflection of its own crisis. Totalitarian regimes are not merely dangerous neighbors and even less some kind of an avant-garde of world progress. Alas, just the opposite: they are the avant-garde of a global crisis of this civilization, first European, then Euro-American, and ultimately global. . . .

It's a great, insightful and thoroughly sobering essay, and I urge you to read the entire piece. Intriguingly, awareness for both Basho and Havel involved their awareness of the reality of the natural world. Do you stop your mad dash through life long enough to get in tune with the natural world? Do you stop and smell the roses? In the middle of checking your Blackberry and the text message from somebody you scarcely know, do you even notice the roses are there? Do you even pause long enough to get in tune with your own health? Slow it down, my friends. Take more time to observe and to meditate on what you observe. Both Basho's and Havel's reflections demonstrate that awareness includes not just seeing *how* things are but *why* they are. True awareness also recognizes the gap between what things are and what they could or even *should* be. Think about that.

Showing Up at Grand Central

Let's take what we learn from Basho and Havel and apply it to each solitary individual back at Grand Central Station. You show up with awareness if you expect to make the journey. You are aware of what time your train leaves, of how fast you can walk, of how long it takes to buy a newspaper. You plan your course accordingly. You walk faster; you skip buying the newspaper. If you're not aware of the change in the time and the change of the track, you'll be at the wrong place at the wrong time without even a newspaper to help you pass the time. You'll worry and you'll spend your time wondering what's going on. To be at the right place at the right time, you have to listen to what the loud speaker says—and it's not always easy to understand. But you have to *get the facts* before taking a new direction.

Henry Browning of the Center for Creative Leadership in Colorado Springs said it clearly:

> *The first step in the development of high performance is the cultivation of awareness. Awareness is the process of becoming an observer of my world and myself.*
>
> *As I become competent at observing myself, I begin to notice the gap between the vision I have of myself and the actions I*

take that are not congruent with that vision. My continued awareness or self-observation will eventually take me to a vantage point from which I can see that my interpretation of myself and life is just that, an interpretation. . . .

When I operate at low levels of awareness, there are few options available to me. I simply cannot "see" many choices. In that mode, I am resentful, angry at life and experienced by others as being dull, stuck or cynical.

As I expand my awareness, I am able to see new possibilities. There are always options and choices available. In this mode I am at peace with life, moving forward with ambition and seen by others as alive, alert, vital and optimistic.

You have to be *aware* to live an extraordinary life. The truth is most people go along unaware. They think this is the way things are, so they live with them. They don't recognize that life is ebbing like dusk in autumn. If they notice the belching smokestack at all, they seldom see beyond a short-term solution to the real reason that smokestack is "soiling the heavens." They don't adequately meditate on why things are that way, and thus they don't see the possibility of change, let alone how to change.

Children who are raised in homes where parents yell at each other think that's the way things are. And they grow up to yell at their children because that's what you do. If the father or the mother of a family is an alcoholic, the other parent often hides the problem and makes excuses for the alcoholic parent, especially if the sober parent tells the child not to tell anyone about the problem. Then the child grows up to hide problems. He is unaware that this is not the best way. It's the only way he knows. It's the way he learned to survive. He will carry the dysfunctional coping patterns into adulthood never being aware of what he's doing.

Speaking of the trains running through Grand Central Station, do you know why most modern trains run on the same standard gauge or track width? The gauge became standard on American railroads because they were built by British engineers. British railroads originally adopted the standard because the carriage tooling was available to make axles that size, which accommodated the ruts of British roads. Guess what. The British roads were originally Roman roads, and the ruts, in many instances, were originally made by Roman chariots pulled by two Roman horses.

A lot of us are going through life unaware that our relationships are mediocre, unaware that our career performance is mediocre, unaware that our lives are ordinary, unaware that there's something wrong or something lacking, unaware that something can be done to make the world better and to make our lives extraordinary. We've gotten onto tracks that others built and we just keep rolling along those same tracks until we die. We're as much in ruts as the tracks originally built for Roman chariots. Unaware.

"A Tipping Point"

Of course, some people are aware and are working hard to build widespread awareness.

Former Vice President Al Gore wrote a book titled *An Inconvenient Truth* and later made a documentary film based on the book, released in June 2006. He talks about the disastrous effects of global warming. Earlier he'd wanted to be president and be able to influence public policy about, among other things, our nation's dependence on fossil fuels and our depletion of forests. When his 2000 bid for the presidency failed, he realized that what he had to do was make the public aware of the disastrous effects on the earth, on wildlife and on humankind that global warming will cause in the next few decades and beyond if we use fossil fuels at our current rate. While other books about the problem had been written, of course, Gore's film was likely to reach additional target audiences, especially young moviegoers.

In his documentary film, Gore shows graphically the U.S. cities that will be under water. He plucks our heartstrings by showing us cartoon polar bears drowning because their ice floes are melting. Al Gore wants us to be aware of the gravity of the situation and equally aware that there is a solution: "We have the technology to change this trend, and we as individuals can make a difference by small changes in our routines. Before anyone of us will make these changes and before any of the science is turned to burning less fossil fuels, we as a people have to be aware."

And awareness is growing. *New York Times* reviewer Michiko Kakutani (May 23, 2006), in reviewing Gore's book uses phrases like "global warming seems to be tiptoeing toward *a tipping point in the public consciousness,*" and "the issue has been *making inroads in the collective imagination.*" In other words, awareness.

People often say a change as profound as Vice President Gore is calling for can't be done; it's too big. However, look at history. In 1964, 44 percent of Americans smoked. Officials told us smoking was bad for our health, but we kept on smoking. It couldn't be changed. But look: When the public became fully aware, the percentage of people who smoked dropped from 43 percent to 22 percent today, not because young people aren't joining the ranks of smokers (they are), but because longer-term smokers are quitting. The already addicted are changing.

The remaining smokers said, it's my business if I smoke or not. I'm not hurting anybody else. Then we became *aware* of the dangers of passive smoking, that second-hand smoke is dangerous to the people around us, especially to our children. And we began to pass laws to prohibit smoking in public places. It used to be people lighted up in our living rooms without even asking. Then they began asking. Now they don't bother asking; they know: If they want to smoke, they go outside. People said it couldn't be done here. And now England is beginning to follow suit, passing laws to reduce smoking in public places. What it took to begin was public awareness.

Learn from Children

Children often seem to be more aware than adults. They take in every new thing around them with keen eyes and ears and taste and touch. They try to make sense of it. They don't know what it means yet, but they are aware. By not knowing what it means yet—what we adults have decided it means—they're able to see things with fresh eyes.

I remember when my grandson Tyler was four years old. He was in the bathtub, lying on his back in about four inches of water. His mom, our daughter Vanessa, was studying at the time, so she was sitting in the bathroom with him, reading and glancing over at him every few seconds. He was lying on his back with all his ducks and boats in the tub, and he said to his mom, "Look, Mom, my penis floats." She didn't want to laugh out loud—that's a guy's worst nightmare even at four—so she said calmly, "Oh, I didn't know that." And he said, in the greatest disgust you can imagine, "Mom, *everybody* knows your penis floats."

He was aware that penises float. He figured everybody was aware. Were you aware that penises float? I wasn't. Maybe I had forgotten because nobody thought it was important. Tyler's observation reminds me that we begin life open-minded and aware, even of the small things. All too soon we learn to ignore and forget and not even see anymore what was once obvious. We must be aware of what is before we can choose what to keep and what to change. We must remember how to look at our life and be aware of what floats and what doesn't!

Barbara Loe Fisher is the president of the National Vaccine Information Center (NVIC) based in Vienna, Virginia, near Washington, D.C. I heard her give a very inspiring talk some years ago. Barbara became interested in vacci-nations after her child went into a coma after a DPT shot and essentially became an autistic child. This was before there was a grass roots movement against immunizations, long before Robert Kennedy, Jr., was on television talk shows talking about it. In 1982, Barbara and another woman, Kathi Williams, put together an organization and began to edu-cate the public on these issues, not to tell them not to vaccinate their children but to educate them about what the risks were before they made that decision. I believe so deeply from the bottom of my heart that people always make the right decisions given the correct informa-tion. They know what is correct and appropriate for them.

Don't bother just to be better than your contemporaries or predecessors. Try to be better than yourself.

WILLIAM FAULKNER

Barbara was trying to make people *aware*, but she was having very little success.

After eight years of working to get an audience who would listen to her, she and her friend were ready to give up. They couldn't go on any longer. Then one day a gentleman in the back of the room was listening to her at one of her talks. He was Dr. Larry Webster, one of the most revered people at Life University in Marietta, Georgia, the man who started the pediatric movement in chiropractic. Dr. Webster went up to her, understanding fully what she was talking about, and invited her down to Life University to speak at a presentation. She didn't want to go. She was done with this campaign. She was going to clear out her office the next week and had no money to do anything. He sent her a plane ticket and brought her down to Georgia where she spoke to a couple hundred chiropractors and found them to be an audience of people who understood and listened.

He sets low personal standards and then consistently fails to achieve them.

PERFORMANCE
EVALUATION

Today because of that experience, the National Vaccine Information Center, a non-profit educational and political advocacy organization, serves as a consumer watchdog on vaccine development and policymaking.

How we show up and *if* we show up at Grand Central Station does make a difference. Barbara Fisher showed up ready to make her life extraordinary. Dr. Webster showed up and met her more than halfway. That chance meeting changed Fisher's life and the lives of millions of kids who have been positively affected by her work.

In 1895, D.D. Palmer, a Canadian practitioner transplanted to Iowa, had an awareness that became the foundation for chiropractic. He encountered an African American man who had been deaf for 17 years. Palmer examined him and found out that he had never damaged his ear and never damaged his brain, but he had damaged his back. Palmer had two wild ideas. His first wild idea was that there was a central controlling mechanism that regulated all body functions including hearing. He thought this central mechanism was the nervous system, but in 1895 he couldn't prove it. He also believed that a body heals itself. What doctors should be trying to do is support that natural process, not override it, he believed.

So Palmer put together these two ideas: The body is a self developing, healing, maintaining mechanism, and the nervous system is critical in how all the parts function. Through your sight, sound, touch, taste and smell your nervous system perceives and adapts you to every change. Palmer learned that the man had heard a "pop" in his back when he'd leaned over and, when he stood up, he was deaf. Palmer noted that the nerves from the back ran through the neck to the brain where the function of hearing is located. So very simply he concluded that since there was nothing wrong with the ears or his brain then there must be some interference with the system that is connecting them. Awareness.

So he laid this man down, found the vertebra out of place in the lower part of his neck, and, the original text says, he "racked" the vertebra back into position. Palmer said the man got up off the table and said he could hear instantaneously. Three days later he was examined medically and had perfectly normal hearing. I had breakfast in Seattle, Washington, with the great-granddaughter of this man. She confirmed that it was well known in her family that he had normal hearing for the rest of his lifetime. What had happened? It would be 30 years later before scientists had enough tools to understand how the nerves connecting his brain and his hearing were disturbed. Palmer simply got rid of a significant interference to the man's nervous system, a spinal misalignment. The adjustment got rid of the interference to the nervous system so the man's body could again function properly. Today 15 million people consult a chiropractor each year, regaining their health without the use of drugs or surgery.

Start a Movement

All the powerful movements in the world started with awareness. There was biologist Rachel Carson who changed the world by writing *Silent Spring*. President John F. Kennedy read the book, published in 1962, and was influenced to call for testing our water for the chemicals mentioned in the book. Carson has been called the mother of the modern environmental movement. Awareness of pollution caused us as a society to move from dumping untreated chemicals into streams to legislation that has cleaned up rivers that once were sewers. Awareness of air pollution has caused us to force automobile manufacturers to find the technology to dramatically reduce harmful emissions from cars. Awareness of the consequences of lead poisoning to children who eat peeling paint or to workmen who sand it caused us to ban the use of lead-based paints in areas available to children and to require workmen to use protective gear when working on surfaces covered with lead-based paint.

There was even time not too far in the past when many people in this country were not aware that slavery was wrong. How could that be? Isn't it obvious? Other people have slaves, why shouldn't we, they said. Without slaves we can't bring the crops in. The slaves are happy. The masters take care of them. Have you ever heard that? Later everyone knew that slavery was utterly wrong, but lots of people thought unequal opportunity was still okay. Unequal was just the way it was. Of course, African-Americans were particularly aware unequal opportunity was wrong, but it took social scientists, Dr. Martin Luther King, Jr., and other activists to make all Americans aware that unequal opportunity was morally wrong and severely damaging to individuals and to society. He made the world aware that racial discrimination was not inevitable; there were things we could do. He made the world aware there was a peaceful solution called law that could change it and that the man in the street could make those in power enact that law.

Dr. Martin Luther King, Jr., addressing participants in a massive march in Washington, D. C., on August 28, 1963, said: "I have a dream that my four little children will one day live in a nation where they will not be judged by the color of their skin but by the content of their character." By stating his dream in a short but eloquent speech, King made us all aware of the possibility many of us never dreamed of. This speech turned the tide and prompted the 1964 Civil Rights Act.

So we open our eyes and our minds, and actually see the way things are and the things that have always been. And by becoming aware we can begin to imagine a better way to live; we can begin to create an extraordinary life.

REFLECT, THEN STEP FORWARD

- The first thing to do to create an extraordinary life is to become aware of what is and the gap between what is and what could be.

- As we expand our awareness we begin to see new options available not only for ourselves but for others in our family, among our friends and in the world at large.

- Keep moving forward, rejecting despair, realizing there comes a "tipping point" where not only your own circumstances but even public consciousness can change dramatically.

PROFILE

Candy Lightner

THE MOTHER WHO REDUCED DRUNK DRIVING

When her 13-year-old daughter was killed by a drunk, hit-and-run driver in 1980, Candy Lightner made herself a promise: "I promised myself on the day of Cari's death that I would fight to make this needless homicide count for something positive in the years ahead."

When the driver was apprehended, it was discovered he had four earlier convictions for DWI. For hitting pedestrian Cari Lightner, this repeat offender received a two-year sentence but avoided prison by serving in a work camp and in a halfway house. Outraged by the leniency of the sentence, Candy Lightner acted on her resolve, organizing Mothers Against Drunk Drivers (MADD) to raise public consciousness about drunk driving and promote tougher legislation against it.

The Californian crusaded across the county, appearing on television, speaking to Congress and business groups, and working zealously for years in behalf of her cause. A television movie in 1983 accelerated the group's growth.

MADD had its greatest success with the enactment of a 1984 federal law that required states to raise the minimum legal age for purchase and possession (but not the drinking age) to 21 or lose federal highway funding. The law was upheld in the

United States Supreme Court in the 1987 case of South Dakota v. Dole.

In 1988 a drunk driver traveling the wrong way on Interstate 71 in Kentucky caused a head-on collision with a school bus. Twenty-seven died, and dozens more were injured in the ensuing fire, one of the worst bus disasters in U.S. history. In the aftermath, more parents swelled the ranks of MADD, and more legislative successes and increased awareness resulted.

MADD claims credit that the death rate from alcohol-related traffic accidents has declined since the 1980s. According to statistics from the National Highway Traffic Safety Administration (NHTSA), alcohol-related traffic deaths per year declined from 26,173 in 1982 to 16,885 in 2005.

As MADD grew over time, temperance forces gained more power within the organization until it largely became anti-alcohol rather than anti-drunk driving, and Ms. Lightner moved on to other things.

Nevertheless, Candy Lightner is credited with changing public consciousness, spearheading legislative change and reducing the likelihood that your loved ones will be killed by a drunk driver. She is indisputably a mother who made a difference.

MAKE YOUR LIFE EX...

CHAPTER   TITLE

GO AHEAD, SHIFT
YOUR PARADIGM

4

:: A PARADIGM IS A BOX
:: EXPERIENCING THE SHIFT
:: SHIFT IN YOUR SHOES
:: PEOPLE DEFEND PARADIGMS AS TRUT...

*Suppose we were able to
share meanings freely without a
compulsive urge to impose our view
or conform to those of others and without distortion and self-deception.
Would this not constitute a real
revolution in culture?*

DAVID BOHM

CHAPTER FOUR

Go Ahead,
Shift Your Paradigm

We are all born in a box, but you don't have to think in it;
in fact, you can act to live outside of it . . . if you choose to.

A PARADIGM IS A MODEL OF REALITY. LET'S SAY YOU WERE A FISH. A fish is conceived in water, born in water, survives in water, eats in water and plays in water. In other words, its basic paradigm of the world is water. It doesn't get up in the morning and say, "Gosh, I have a lot of decisions to make today, but all my decisions are dictated by the fact that I live in water." The fish sees a worm wiggling in the water. With a stroke of his fins and a flop of his tail, he zooms over to the worm without a thought and simply snaps it up. If he's lucky, life goes on. If he's unlucky, the worm is attached to a hook and a line, and the fish is hauled up out of the water, where the fish's basic paradigm of life in water is useless and none of his behaviors based on that paradigm work.

Sometimes that happens to us humans; we are hauled out of our element. Most of the time, though, we just go along living according to our paradigms, not thinking about them. While our various paradigms serve as our models of reality—how we see the world—and they control our behavior, we don't very often think *about* them any more than the fish does. We think *from* them.

Because our paradigms control our behavior, we behave *from* our paradigms.

Let me give you another example. I saw a story on television about two girls who have a condition whereby they can't be exposed to sunlight or ultraviolet radiation of any kind. If they are exposed to sunlight or ultraviolet light even through a window, they will get cancer because their skin cells can't repair the damage. They stay in the house in the daytime. If someone comes to their house, they have to be in a different room until the visitor has come in and shut the door because even the sunlight coming through the front door would kill them within a short time. The only time they go out is late at night. All they see of the world is night. Their view of the world must be very different from ours. They think from fear of sunlight, from fragile health, from a dark outside world. Their behavior of caution and avoidance comes from their paradigm or view of the world.

The fish's wet world and the girls' dark world seem foreign to most of us. Yet we all have paradigms, our own complex views of the world, shaped mostly by the culture we were raised in.

A man named John Grinder, along with colleague Richard Bandler, developed a group concept called Neurolinguistics Programming or NLP. NLP focuses on how subjective reality drives beliefs, perceptions and behaviors. John Grinder speaks 17 languages. He believes that our models of reality are built and perpetuated by the language that we use. Because we each speak in a particular language, not only is our sentence structure different but how we view the world is different. There's a model of reality, that is, a paradigm we can call "Being French." There's a model of reality we can call "Being Russian." There's a model of reality we can call "Being Australian." There's a model of reality we can call "Being American."

It's not just a change in accent; it's that different nationalities actually see the world differently, based on language, on their culture and on how they were raised.

Olga Grushin, a Moscow native and a 1993 graduate of Emory University, wrote a novel titled *The Dream Life of Sukhanov*, published in January 2006, which has been favorably reviewed in major newspapers. Although she didn't come to the English-speaking world until her freshman year at Emory, Grushin wrote this first novel in English; it was not only a change of language; it was a major paradigm shift for her. Early in her college career she had been allowed to write her Russian-lit papers in Russian. Then one day a professor suggested she rewrite a Russian paper in English. Grushin did and realized that it was a very different paper. The professor "suggested that her English might in fact be more direct and personal than her Russian." Her native language reflected the "personality" of her native culture, while her second language, English, had a different personality, one that was more "direct and personal." [Alec T. Young, *Emory Magazine*, Spring 2006, "Precis," p. 6.]

> *To change one's life:*
>
> *1. Start immediately,*
>
> *2. Do it flamboyantly,*
>
> *3. No exceptions.*
>
> WILLIAM JAMES

Obviously, not all Americans or Russians or French are the same. They're not raised the same, so certainly in one nationality there are different paradigms. In the U.S., the Kennedy family of Boston is American, and they think from the paradigm of what an American is. They are also Irish-American and that is a distinctive culture also, so they think from being Irish-American. The Kennedy's adhere to another even more specialized paradigm—a family of presidential material. The patriarch Joseph Kennedy groomed his oldest son Joe to be president. When Joe was killed in an airplane crash, the role—

and paradigm—of presidential candidate fell to Jack Kennedy. After President Kennedy was assassinated, his brother Robert Kennedy took up the torch and ran for president. The youngest brother, Ted, felt pressure to do the same because being presidential material was the family paradigm. The family knew the formula, had the support and counted on the charisma, but Robert's assassination put a damper on that idea—changed the paradigm—and Ted, who had gotten as far as the Senate, remained there. Maria Shriver, a niece of Jack, Robert and Ted, married a man who later became governor of California, and naturally, because she's a Kennedy, everybody wonders if the U.S. Constitution will be changed to allow her foreign-born husband to run for president. I believe that every Kennedy considers becoming president. It's part of the Kennedy paradigm.

In your family, perhaps your mother said to you as you left home for a special event, "Have a good time and remember who you are." What was she talking about? She was talking about your family paradigm. In my childhood, I was supposed to behave like a Riekeman, and you were supposed to behave like whatever your family paradigm prescribed.

Sometimes the outside world knows your paradigm or thinks they do. "Oh, you're one of the Riekeman boys," someone might say. And if we were good boys, they would assume we were good and I'd try my best to be good. And if we were slackers, people would assume we were all slackers, and we'd behave pretty much the way we were expected because that's what we expected of ourselves also. We'd think from the paradigm of slackers.

A Paradigm Is a Box

A paradigm defines the limits of the world as you know it. To make a paradigm shift, you become aware of some new and meaningful facts outside the box. In other words, you think outside of the box. In the last chapter, about awareness, I reminded you of some people who have become aware. When they became aware of new facts and the possibilities those facts offered, they became able to think outside the box. When thinking leads to action, a shift occurs. The people I cited all followed up on their awareness and acted. I have to make an exception of my grandson; I'm not sure that he has acted on his awareness of what part of his anatomy floats. But most of them acted on their awareness and spearheaded change. That's how we even know of them.

But awareness, while crucial to living an extraordinary life, is not all you must do. *Acting* on your awareness is also necessary. When Al Gore became aware of the dangers of global warming and thinking from that relatively new paradigm, he shifted his energy to reducing fossil fuel use and deforestation. He ran for president with this shift as part of his platform. Failing to win the presidency, he focused on enlarging public awareness to the tipping point where the public would demand change of its leaders.

Awareness comes first and action comes second. But it's not easy because the folks in the box with us, who think from the paradigm the box represents, don't want to shift. Thinking from the paradigm, they don't see another way. Often, as I've mentioned before, the very young are not initially bound by the paradigm; they are aware from their own fresh vision. But the folks in the paradigm do all they can to keep the children in the box, to train them in the paradigm. Harry Chapin's song "Flowers are Red" tells a little story of how we are shaped from childhood to stay in the box, to think from our culture's paradigm.

In the song, a little boy went to school where he took his crayons and drew flowers and leaves of many different colors. The teacher said,

> *Flowers are red, young man*
> *Green leaves are green*
> *There's no need to see flowers any other way*
> *Than the way they've always been seen.*

The little boy protested that there are so many other colors, but the teacher drummed the refrain into his head until "finally he got lonely/frightened thoughts filled his head" and he capitulated. Like many children, the boy was aware, but he soon parroted the paradigm of his culture. He confined himself to the box.

Not every paradigm shift changes the world or has a lasting impact. Consider New Coke or your brother-in-law's invention of a perpetual motion machine. However, one thing is certain: The awareness that allows you to live an extraordinary life is awareness that allows a paradigm shift. Action follows that shift.

Experiencing the Shift

There's an exercise I use in some of my seminars so that participants can feel a paradigm shift, on a small scale. If you know what it feels like, you can recognize it when it hits you. If you know what you're looking for, you can move toward it. In fact, this exercise can give you the feel of a paradigm shift in less than a minute.

Here's how it works. I ask everyone in the audience to find a partner and to sit with a chair between them. Then I ask each of them to put an elbow on the back of the chair between them and prepare to arm wrestle. I give them these instructions: You have 15 seconds from the time I say go. I want you to wrestle full-out for the entire 15 seconds. When one of you pins your partner, wrestle again. Every time you pin the other person, you win a million dollars. The objective is to win as much money as you can.

I say, "Go!" and they are off. They brace themselves and grunt and groan for 15 seconds until I say, "Stop!"

Then I ask how many people won no money? There may be a few. I ask how many people won less than five million. Most of them raise their hands. "Anyone in here with more than five million?" I ask. There is sometimes someone who won, let's say, 16 million. His partner has won about the same. Everyone is amazed. If one partner won 16 million, someone always asks, doesn't the other one have to lose?

A person starts to live when he can live outside himself.

ALBERT EINSTEIN

According to the paradigm of arm wrestling we all know, yes, someone has to lose if the other one wins. And you don't want to be the one to lose, so you gear up to pin the other guy. You do your best to pin him. That's the way the game is played. That's the paradigm of arm wrestling.

What did I say was the objective of this game? To win money. Most of the participants replaced that objective with "Pin 'em!"

However, two people decided to cooperate with each other instead of fight, and they went back and forth pinning each other without resistance as fast as they could so that they could each win as much as possible. Scoring about one pin per second each, they won 16 million dollars a piece. These two people didn't act on the most commonly understood paradigm of arm wrestling—competition.

They were *aware* that there were other, more rewarding possibilities.

The greatest thing you could bring with you to Grand Central Station is awareness. Once you know what it feels like, you can recognize a possible shift and act on it. You can seek it out.

Scientists seek it out all the time. They start out perhaps following traditional paths, but when they get blocked they ask themselves, is there another way of looking at this? The person who coined the phrase "paradigm shifts" was in fact speaking of science. Science historian Thomas Kuhn coined the phrase in his 1962 book *The Structure of Scientific Revolutions*. He said that science does not progress by the accumulation of new knowledge, but by periodic revolutions he called paradigm shifts, in which the nature of scientific inquiry within a particular field is abruptly transformed. Other people who typically are aware enough to identify and publicize paradigm shifts are marketers, advertisers and entrepreneurs.

Shift in Your Shoes

Here are some classic paradigm shifts of modern times. When I was growing up, I had to go to gym class every school day. Because of the weather, half the year we had to be in the gym. That's why we called it gym class. Because they didn't want you to wreck the gym floor with gritty street shoes, we were required to wear special canvas shoes with rubber-soles called "gym shoes." The only time we wore those rubber-soled shoes was to gym class. We had a special locker to keep our gym shoes in because they didn't even want us carrying the shoes outside because we might get grit on them. Did we get to wear them to the mall? No. Did we get to wear them to church? No. Where I came from, we'd go to hell if we wore our gym shoes to church. So there was a limited market for these shoes. The market was junior high and high school kids to wear for an hour every day for something called gym class.

The paradigm of gym shoes, like all paradigms, had consequences associated with it, and it had possibilities. The consequence of gym shoes for gym class was that there were only two mass-market gym shoe companies because the market was not very big. There was the expensive gym shoe for the serious athlete—Converse. And Converse gym shoes only came in two styles, high-tops and low-tops, blacks and whites. The other gym shoe was for wimps. This shoe had been around since 1917. It was the shoe you dreaded that your mother would buy you one day while you were at school because they were cheaper—Keds. So there were Converse and Keds, two kinds of gym shoes.

Then someone came along who was aware of other possibilities. This person said we can have different shoes for different sports and we can call them sports shoes. And we said, "Okay." Did anybody argue with them? No. Look at the outcome: Sports shoes as opposed to gym shoes. The sports shoe industry is now a 15-billion-dollar-a-year industry. That's one of the outcomes of the paradigm shift from gym shoes to sports shoes. There is a sports shoe that's for tennis. And that's different from the sports shoe for running, which is different from the sports shoe for walking, which is different from the sports shoe for basketball, which is different from the sports shoe for court games like squash and racquetball. If you do a lot of those activities, you may want to buy a cross-trainer that offers aspects of each one of the other sports shoes. That's a paradigm shift, from gym shoes in two styles and two colors to sports shoes that gave jobs to hundreds of graphic designers every season who added colors, textures and graphics. Swooshes and slogans came fast behind. That was a paradigm shift in the canvas-shoe-with-rubber-sole industry.

Here's another: Someone came along who said, "Sports shoes are fashion footwear." Again, we said okay. So now there's the sports shoe you wear with your jeans on Saturday nights. Then there's the $100 sports shoe that women wear with $1,000 dollar Armani business suits because no woman would wear high heels out on the street to walk to work anymore. I've seen them with high-tops and low-tops and even without a heel: a slide, almost like a sandal, still made of canvas and rubber soles, gym shoes but missing some parts.

They come in black and white and a zillion other colors like fuchsia, peach, lemon meringue, slate and choco-

A prejudiced person is one who doesn't believe in the same things we do.

ART LINKLETTER

late. I've seen sports shoes with sequins, with beads and with cartoon characters painted on them. How many of you have just one pair in your closet? And how many of you use that one pair just for gym class? We've seen more than one paradigm shift since I first wore gym shoes, and now we're thinking *from* the current paradigm. My collaborator Letitia says even her 85-year-old mother complained about a gift of trim leather shoes, what she called "old lady" shoes. Instead, she wanted Nikes with the swoosh. Why? It wasn't so she could protect a gym floor. Her wishes arose *from* the paradigm of sports-shoes-are-cool. Because somebody said so.

Here's another example. Do you remember when water used to be free? You'd come home from school and you'd look in the refrigerator, "Ah shoot. No soda pop, no Hawaiian punch, no iced tea. I guess I have to have *water.*" Then someone came along and said, "Water, elegant drink, chic restaurants." We said, "Okay." And they said, "Great! $1.50 for six ounces." And they put them in neat little bottles and created a multi-billion-dollar industry by just getting us to change how we view water. Water is a gourmet item instead of a basic thirst quencher. Now we have to carry a bottle of store-bought water everywhere, water as a fashion statement. We complain about $3-a-gallon gasoline, but we're willing to pay $8 a gallon for water. Now that's a paradigm shift!

People Defend Paradigms as Truth

How long did the communists defend communism as if it were truth? Forty years? They built walls. They had big missiles and nuclear warheads, and so did we. Wow! That's a paradigm. I'd say it had some major consequences on us all. Then all of a sudden one year, this paradigm called communism just shriveled up. The communists just voted themselves out of power.

Who could have guessed that the paradigm would have shifted like that in one year? If I'd told you two years before that next year the communists were going to vote themselves out of power because communism was a bankrupt system, you would have said, "You must be crazy." In the twinkling of an eye, we had a different paradigm.

You raise your children. Where did you learn to raise your children? Somebody just made it up. Who made it up? You made most of it up, didn't you? You may say, "Well, no, I got a lot of it from my parents." So true. And where did they get it? They got it from their parents. And where did their parents get it? At some point in the past somebody did what? They just made it up.

A woman I know has raised four well-behaved children. She says her own parents spanked her occasionally and she heard them often criticize other parents, those who had a badly behaved child, saying, "What that child needs is a good spanking." They defended the paradigm of spanking. My friend grew up thinking it was neglectful to fail to spank misbehaving children. She therefore spanked her first two children occasionally until they learned what kind of behavior was required. Nine years later she had two more children. Experts had started advising parents not to spank children, saying that spanking taught children to use violence and the power of size in their own lives, and that there were better ways of disciplining children. So my friend didn't spank her two younger children. The paradigm had changed from her parents' paradigm to a new paradigm. Why? Because somebody said so. But all four kids, the ones spanked and those not spanked, all grew up just fine.

We can't easily understand another paradigm from the paradigm we're in because we don't think *about* these paradigms, we think *from* them. A paradigm controls our behavior. How we view sports shoes and water is not something we created. Where then do these paradigms come from? Here's the answer. Somebody just made them up. Karl Marx just made up communism. Where did canvas and rubber shoes as fashion footwear or canvas and rubber shoes as gym shoes come from? The answer is somebody just made it up.

How come paradigms continue when we know that somebody just made them up? The answer is, we perpetuate them. The way paradigms continue is we continue them on automatic pilot. We continue a paradigm until somebody makes up something different. Until somebody says something else is so.

You can be that person. First, you become aware of the paradigm you are acting *from* and you become aware that there are other, better possibilities. Then you decide which of these possibilities you want to become reality and you *say so*. You can be the one. In later chapters of this book, I'm going to tell you how to become that person.

PATHWAYS TO CHANGE

- We're all born into, and usually stay in, a paradigm or way of looking at the world. To create an extraordinary life we have to consider seeing and acting differently.

- Paradigms shift all around us—like gym shoes becoming sports shoes. We act extraordinarily when we think outside the box of the current paradigm, imagine other possibilities, then act to fulfill them.

- Rather than simply perpetuating whatever paradigm you're experiencing, realize that somebody just said so and the paradigm formed. Well, once you become aware, **you** can say so and shift to a new paradigm. Think and live outside the box.

MAKE YOUR LIFE EXT...

KEEP THINGS NEW—ALWAYS

CHAPTER   TITLE

5

:: PHASE TWO

:: PHASE THREE

:: HOW THE NEW PARADIGM WORKS

:: CHANGING YOUR UNDERWEAR.

*The creation of something new
is not accomplished by the intellect
but by the play instinct acting from
inner necessity. The creative mind
plays with the objects it loves.*

CARL JUNG

CHAPTER FIVE

Keep Things New—Always

The new paradigm begins with exciting opportunity,
but be careful. Success can spoil anything.

———

PARADIGMS GO THROUGH THREE DIFFERENT STEPS OR PHASES. In the first phase of a paradigm, someone creates a new model of reality like racial equality or chiropractic or fashion foot-wear. *Wow*, you think. *Wish I'd thought of that!* Or maybe you are the one who created the new model. You are the one who became aware of the paradigm you were operating *from*, and you saw other, better possibilities, and you shifted to a new paradigm. *Wow! This is great!* you think. *The sky's the limit!*

A new paradigm is heady stuff. In that new model of the world you see unlimited opportunity, possibility and potential. For example, imagine that in the old paradigm you weren't in love; you spent your life looking for love or hanging out with your pals; you were acting from the paradigm of "unattached." Then you fell in love. Everything changed.

You're now acting from a new paradigm, that of being in a romantic relationship. You don't know much about that paradigm at first. You can't even figure out how to fulfill a relationship and all the things that go on in a relationship until you get into one. People all around you talk about relationships, but you don't know what they're talking about until you are in one. When you first fall in love, you expect the relationship to go perfectly because you're in love. Think again. How many of you are in relationships and you've never had any problems? Always been perfect? No misunderstandings? Never had any arguments? Everybody was clear? You've always been in love the way you were the first day you met? Anybody? I didn't think so. You can't very well figure out what the answers to the problems in a relationship are until you get into one. When you get into any new paradigm, it looks like there are unlimited possibilities—and there are.

Starting a new business or professional practice, taking up a new hobby or sport, relocating, acting with confidence instead of timidity, or making any other major change in your life is a lot like falling in love. It's a whole new ball game. It's exciting and the possibilities stretch out into the future without limits.

Phase Two

The second phase of the paradigm begins when we figure out how to function in the new paradigm. That's where we learn the rules. That's where we make them work. You put a lot of energy into your business and get little return for it. You put a lot of work into your new fitness program and for a while you see no results. You spend a lot of time filling a sales pipeline before you ever see the profits. Then you learn the ropes and figure out the rules. And now you can put out less energy and get more results. That's the second phase.

Let's take D.D. Palmer, the father of chiropractic. As a doctor of chiropractic myself, I speak to a lot of chiropractors and I use chiropractic in a lot of my examples. The history of chiropractic is certainly a good model of changing paradigms.

D.D. Palmer was a 19th century teacher, beekeeper and rasp-berry grower in several towns along the Mississippi river. In the 1880s he was influenced by a "magnetic healer" to become a practitioner himself. He opened the Palmer Cure and Infirmary in Davenport, Iowa, in 1887. One day two years later, you may remember, he became aware that one of his patients, who had been deaf for 17 years, did not have a problem with his ears or his brain but that he had lost his hearing at the exact moment of a "popping" in his neck. Here's where a paradigm shift followed awareness. Palmer realized the obstruction in the man's spine was blocking the neural pathways that connected the brain and ear to the rest of the body. Palmer adjusted his spine, and the man's hearing was immediately restored. Healing was something the body does naturally if obstruction is removed, Palmer reasoned. A new paradigm, Phase One. Palmer renamed his clinic the Palmer School and Infirmary of Chiropractic. The sky was the limit. He found that his "hand corrections" relieved the symptoms of many different kinds of illnesses, and he taught chiropractic to students. As he moved into Phase Two, his practice thrived and chiropractic became a tradition with all the rules understood.

> *To keep our faces toward change, and behave like free spirits in the presence of fate, is strength undefeatable.*
>
> HELEN KELLER

Many of you chiropractors out there as well as other business owners, artists, teachers, salesmen, lawyers and engineers are out there in Phase Two, learning the rules, applying them, getting your practice into a position where you carry on indefinitely with less effort than in the early days.

And what lies ahead? Phase Three. Maybe you're already there.

Phase Three

The third phase of a paradigm—it could be the longest phase—is where all the possibilities are used up. Whether you work in construction or have a professional career, in Phase Three you've honed your skills and know how to make your business work. You do that for 10 years. Gradually, you settle into a rut, and you do that for the next 30 years of your life. All the possibilities are used up, and you don't see your way out of it because you are not even *aware* of it. You don't think about the paradigm of doing your work the way you've always done it. You don't think *about* it, you think *from* it. You know the rules, you can get by.

The funny thing is that the third phase is usually where most of the money is, in a business situation. You think, "Man, this is going great! This is wonderful!" And then one day you hit the wall. All of a sudden one day, because you haven't created anything new, the excitement, purpose, creativity and energy die. And then you're on the beach. I've been there.

This is also where many marriages wind up because the couple doesn't create anything new in that relationship. They don't see any new possibilities. I'm not talking about seeking new relationships. I'm talking about the current one they're in where they've figured out how to get by.

"Getting by" is the hallmark of Phase Three. I'm writing this to tell you that when you are just getting by, your entire life is already over. The possibilities are all used up. You know it, and you're walking around not letting anybody see that your life is bankrupt. Unless you create some new possibilities, your work life is finished. Your relationship is done. Your interests are boring. There's nothing left in any of them for you any longer. You're doing some coasting and there are some good moments, but there's nothing new available for you in life.

If you don't create something new, your business is going to die and your relationships already have. What you're reading is about how to create some new possibilities. We're talking about recapturing your lives, about getting yourself into Grand Central Station with awareness, about leaning forward that one inch, putting forth that one extra degree of effort that will make your life extraordinary.

Let me remind you of what happened in chiropractic. Palmer's original paradigm shift, Phase One, gave him unlimited possibilities. His practice became a successful movement. His descendants continued in the family profession, defining the rules and refining practice in Phase Two. The family institution became Palmer College of Chiropractic in 1961 as more science education moved chiropractic toward the mainstream of health care. Here's where chiropractic was reaping the rewards; health insurance was paying for patients' care, and the field was growing.

The key in racing is either to be accelerating or braking—never just coasting along. It's when you're coasting that you have the least amount of control.

KHARI VILLELA

For well over a century, chiropractic has been relieving pain and improving health. There were some new inventions and new procedures along the way, but in one important way chiropractic practice was always pretty much the same. The patients came, they got better, and they left. The doctor-patient relationship was temporary. Somewhere along the way, the relationship between patient and chiropractic went into Phase Three.

In the paradigm from which chiropractors and patients were operating, if a patient comes into the chiropractor's office with low back pain, he doesn't want to stay very long, and he wants to pay as little as possible, preferably nothing. How long is he going to stick around? The average number of visits nationally for patients coming into that kind of practice might be six to seven visits. And when would they drop out? When they don't hurt any more. Their paradigm about health is that they're healthy if they don't hurt. How do people know when they're healthy? When they feel good. How do they know when they're sick? When they feel bad. So do we ever have patients calling us up because they feel great? No. They call us up because they hurt. They stop coming when they don't hurt. Unless you can shift the paradigm of health from which they operate, they're going to be gone in six or seven visits. They don't come in to maintain health and to prevent problems.

My wife is the sweetest, most tolerant, most beautiful woman in the world. This is a paid political announcement.

HENNY YOUNGMAN

For a hundred years most chiropractors accepted the paradigm of the temporary patient. We've been operating in Phase Three of D.D. Palmer's paradigm, which was new in 1899. We are programmed to function within a certain pattern of behavior, and we don't get out of it. Where do these paradigms come from? Somebody made them up. And who perpetuates them? We do. And if you want to change them, you have to say so.

In the 1970s, I wasn't the only one who had become aware of another possibility. But when my paradigm of chiropractic practice shifted to wellness and prevention as well as caring for patients with symptoms, I did something many others did not—I said so. I authored and produced chiropractic patient education videotapes, children's programs, public service announcements, commercials and TV shows for use in the national media. I partnered with people who were more in the public eye than I was to bring the message to patients and lay audiences around the world. I am proud to be a part of the wellness healthcare revolution, a new paradigm that replaced the old paradigm of the temporary patient.

How the New Paradigm Works

Some people consider me an expert in patient education. I'm not into patient education; I'm into patient paradigm shifting. One of the first shifts I try to create is the understanding that health has to do with how you are and not necessarily how you feel. For example, if you eat some bad food and you start throwing up, you might feel bad but throwing up is a sign that your body is working properly and getting rid of a toxin so it doesn't do more damage to your body. On the other hand, you can feel great but, if you have early-stage cancer, you are not healthy. The first shift in our relationship with patients has got to be from talking about *how you feel* to talking about *how you are* and how you are functioning. And then chiropractic becomes a matter of helping people *be* healthier and functioning better as opposed to just *feeling* better. As long as chiropractic lives in the realm of feeling better, patients are going to drop out after six or seven visits.

Let me show you an example. A woman walked into a chiropractor's office in Connecticut, complaining of neck pain and low back pain. She was having pain down her arm, brachial neuralgia. She had some numbness and tingling in her fingers in the morning when she got up. She also had a condition called "foot drop," which is paralysis of the anterior tibialis, the muscle on the front of the calf. When you take a step forward, your toe is supposed to stay up so it doesn't flop and you're not tripping on it all the time. But if that muscle is paralyzed, your foot flops. So the chiropractor took X-rays. Instead of her neck curving forward, it was curving backwards in the opposite direction. She had about a 400 percent loss of the cervical curve. So the chiropractor looked at this and put her under care. Within four weeks all of her symptoms were gone, including the foot drop, and none of those conditions or symptoms ever came back again.

At the end of four weeks, her husband was transferred, and they left town. Nine months later they came back. The woman still had no symptoms, but the chiropractors had done some good education with her earlier, and she decided to go back in and see them. Because it had been 10 months since the original exam, they thought they'd better X-ray her again. The new X-rays looked pretty much like the old ones. There was still a significant loss of curve. A few weeks or months of chiropractic care can get rid of a patient's symptoms, but the spine itself may still not be working properly. You may say, so what? If the spine isn't functioning normally, it will always have a resulting neuro-logical damage or deficit to the nervous system. This woman still had neurological damage. And since the nervous system is what controls how the body functions, symptomatic or not, there's still damage. In this case the patient was not healthy. Her body was not functioning properly. So the doctor put her into spinal reconstructive care and seven weeks later they X-rayed her again. Her lateral cervical curve was not perfect but pretty close.

I'm saying that you can feel good and still not be healthy. And that, until a patient has a paradigm shift about health and its relation-ship to proper function, then nothing you're going to do or say to them is going to make any difference.

However, I'm not just talking about how to have a good business. I'm not just talking about how a chiropractor can have increased patient visits. I'm not just talking about how he or she can have less dependency on new patients or insurance companies. What I'm talking about is giving patients optimum health care and teaching them to live at 100 percent.

To live at 100 percent, to live an extraordinary life, you have to have a paradigm shift in every area of your life: in your business and in all your relationships—with your parents, your spouse, your children, your neighbors and your clients. I contend that the paradigm shift is a small shift that in the twinkling of the eye alters how we look at the world.

Changing Your Underwear

Let me give you an example of a paradigm from one of the great philosophers of our time. I love philosophy. I love reading Aristotle and Ayn Rand, but I believe the greatest philosopher of our time appears twice a night on television reruns in many cities; it's Norm on *Cheers*.

Norm has a paradigm that we all understand. Norm's paradigm is beer and that barstool, which he sits on through every show. All of his decisions are based on beer and sitting on that barstool. He never gets outside that paradigm. Here comes Norm into the bar. Since everybody understands his paradigm, as soon as he opens up the door, Sam is pouring a beer. And he puts the beer at the end of the bar where Norm's stool is. That's how these paradigms work. We don't think *about* them, we think *from* them. So Norm comes walking in and the whole bar hollers out, "Normy" with their Boston accents. He heads down to the end of the bar. As he passes Sam, Sam says to him, "Norm, how's the world treating you?" And Norm's response is "Sammy, it's a dog-eat-dog world out there, and I'm wearing Milk Bone underwear." That's his paradigm. It never shifts.

Norm's right. It is a dog-eat-dog world out there. There are people out there who may take your children. There are people out there who may cause you not to get home to your family tonight because they're drunk and they run a traffic light and kill you. There's nothing you can do about it. There are people out there in third-world countries that unleash chemical weapons on people in their own country and kill whole communities of people because they don't like them. It is a dog-eat-dog world out there. The question is, What is your relationship to it going to be?

Someone asked me in an interview one time what my seminars were about and I didn't have time to explain and I said, "Well, it's a seminar in which people change their underwear."

What you and I do here has the possibility of changing the world. What must change is your relationship to it. Your spouse is not going to be different when you get home tonight. What can change are the possibilities that you see in your spouse when you get there. Your business is not going to be different next week. The colleague you can't stand is going to be waiting for you at work tomorrow. What can change is your relationship with him. And if our relationships and how we view the world can shift and change enough, then the world can change, too. It changed from Communist countries to countries trying to build free market economies. It changed in the twinkling of an eye. It changed from a couple of companies selling gym shoes to high school kids to a $15-billion-dollar-a-year industry. And it changed how? Just because people said so. If you want a different relationship with your spouse, you want to double your business, you want a different relationship with your staff and your friends, all this can change just because you say so. If you doubt that your say-so is that powerful, read on.

KEEP THINGS FRESH

- When you get to Phase Three of anything—from a business to a relationship—the newness tends to get lost, and when things aren't new and growing, they're dying.

- Short of changing careers or finding a different romantic relationship, investigate possibilities to do things differently, perhaps dramatically so, in order to get the creative juices flowing.

- Obviously there are things about the world we can't change. What we can change is our relationship to it, and that new relationship and what we say to others about it, can make a huge difference in our lives and the lives around us.

PROFILE
Jody Williams
Fighting to Ban Land Mines Around the World

Jody Williams won the Nobel Peace Prize in 1997 for her tireless opposition to governments' use of landmines, which remain buried throughout the world, posing threat of death or loss of limbs to millions of civilians.

The feisty Vermont woman developed empathy for human frailty as she watched school children taunt her disabled brother. Later experiences further molded her passion to correct human rights violations as she protested the Vietnam War, taught in an English as a Second Language program in Mexico, and developed an interest in U.S. policy on Central America.

She launched her career fighting for humanitarian causes from 1984-86 as coordinator of the Nicaragua-Honduras Education Project, leading fact-finding delegations from the region. Her efforts continued as she became the deputy director of the Los Angeles-based Medical Aid for El Salvador, spearheading relief efforts for the organization from 1986-92. With encouragement from the Vietnam Veterans of America Foundation, she began to mobilize the movement to ban landmines.

Conceptualized in 1991 by Williams and several non-governmental groups, the International Campaign to Ban Landmines (ICBL) has grown from six founding organizations to a network of more than 1,100 human rights, medical, arms control, environmental, women's, and children's organizations from more than 60 countries.

In accepting the Nobel Prize, Williams called attention to the insidious danger of landmines: "Landmines distinguish themselves because once they have been sown, once the soldier walks away from the weapon, the landmine cannot tell the difference between a soldier or a civilian—a woman, a child, a grandmother going out to collect firewood to make the family meal. The crux of the problem is that while the use of the weapon might be militarily justifiable during ... even the two months of the battle, once peace is declared the landmine does not recognize that peace. The landmine is eternally prepared to take victims ... The war ends, the landmine goes on killing."

The Nobel Committee, which awarded the peace prize to Williams and the ICBL, said that the ICBL's work "has grown into a convincing example of an effective policy for peace." Williams, who directed the campaign from 1991-97, now is the organization's international ambassador, advocating for increased efforts and funding to clear unexploded mines and provide assistance to victims.

By 1999, the ICBL's push for the Mine Ban Treaty—which prohibits the use, production, stockpiling, or transfer of these mines—became international law.

*Leadership is not magnetic
personality—that can just as well
be a glib tongue. It is not "making
friends and influencing people"—that is
flattery. Leadership is lifting a person's vision
to higher sights, the raising of a person's
performance to a higher standard, the
building of a personality beyond
its normal limitations.*

PETER F. DRUCKER

CHAPTER SIX

You *Must* Become a Leader

Leaders are made, not born, and you may be surprised
what they are and are not made of.

———

Y OU MAY THINK THAT YOUR "SAYING SO" DOESN'T HAVE MUCH
power outside of your household and sometimes not even
there. Maybe you'd like to tend to your own backyard, live in
the old tried and true paradigm, and let someone else lead.

You may say some people are cut out to be leaders from the
beginning, and you aren't one of them. You may think that leaders are
born with some advantage you don't have. Renowned leadership
researchers Warren Bennis and Burt Nanus disagree. In their book
Leaders,* Bennis and Nanus said: "The most dangerous leadership
myth is that leaders are born—that there is a genetic factor to leadership. This myth asserts that people simply either have certain
charismatic qualities or not. That's nonsense; in fact, the opposite is
true. Leaders are made rather than born."

If leadership is not inherited genetically and it's "made," then
what is it made of? Connections? Money? Education?

In *Leaders,* you'll find the results of the most comprehensive study
on leadership conducted in our society. In their 15-year study, Bennis
and Nanus followed 90 of the top corporate executives from Fortune

500 companies and other leaders like the head of a symphony and several heads of state. In some cases, they actually moved, for up to a year, into the homes of people who were considered to be leaders to see if they lived differently. Did they eat differently? Did they talk differently? What kind of television did they watch? The researchers looked for everything that might have anything to do with leadership and here are some of the things they found:

1. Leadership Has Nothing to Do with "Who You Know"

A lot of people think, if we could just meet the right people, if we could just hobnob with prominent people, then we could put our business, our profession, and our life on the map. Look at some of the great leaders throughout history, like Mohandas Gandhi, who pioneered nonviolent resistance and won India's independence from foreign domination. He led movements for civil rights for poor farmers and laborers, women and the lowest social class, the untouchables, fighting against the injustices imposed by the class into which he was born. Look at Rosa Parks, a black woman in Montgomery, Alabama, who led the bus boycott in 1955 that was a major turning point for the civil rights movement. An obscure seamstress, she became a leader by sitting on that bus and refusing to get off because she had a vision of equal rights for black people. These people were outside the "who-you-need-to-know" system. In fact, what they were trying to do was overthrow the "who-you-need-to-know" system, working for and with the unknowns and the untouchables. Leadership has nothing to do with "who you know."

The very essence of leadership is that you have to have vision. You can't blow an uncertain trumpet.

THEODORE M. HESBURGH

2. Leadership Has Nothing to Do with Money

I "googled" the words "came from poverty," and I found over 9,000 sources of the words. Hundreds of them were talking about people, little known or well known, whose visions may or may not agree with yours but who were definitely leaders and they "came from poverty."

I found reports on Luiz Inacio Lula da Silva, elected president of Brazil in 2003, born in poverty. I found famous writers like African-American playwright August Wilson, experts like sociologist Marta Tienda, and actors like Charlie Chaplin, leaders and innovators in their fields, all born in poverty. Dale Carnegie, who introduced 30 million readers to self-improvement via his book *How to Win Friends and Influence People* and his Dale Carnegie courses, was born poor on a farm in Missouri.

The obituaries of every newspaper are filled with people who were raised poor and ended up influential leaders, for example, the *New York Times* obituary of Aaron Solomon Sadove, of Jamesport, New York, who died in April 2006. Sent during World War II to China, Burma and India to build air supply routes over the Himalayas to support the fight against the Japanese in China, he became a leader, retiring as a full colonel. In civilian life, he became Senior Vice President of Con Edison, and in retirement he continued to be a leader. The obituary says he "became a rock of the community . . . and, among other things, established a professional fundraising program for Eastern Long Island Hospital. Aaron was a man of passionate commitment to fairness and integrity. He never forgot that he came from poverty." A life-long leader, in other words, who began life without money.

And here's a quotation about poverty from Gleason L. Archer, an educator who founded Suffolk School of Law, an evening school designed to "serve ambitious young men who are obliged to work for a living while studying law." Archer said, "History has demonstrated that the great leaders of every age were, almost without exception, born in poverty, denied educational advantages in boyhood, and obliged to educate themselves at odd moments while doing a man's work in the world. The same immutable principle is in operation today—the earnest souls who now toil in the evening schools to fit themselves for life will be found in the front ranks of our civilization of tomorrow."

Gleason L. Archer himself worked his way through college and law school before founding Suffolk School of Law. Its first graduate to pass the Bar was a machinist by trade. If Archer was speaking today, he would say great leaders were denied advantages in "childhood" instead of "boyhood" and they would do an "adult's work" in the world instead of a "man's work," but he was speaking in 1923. It would take other leaders to expand the paradigm of leadership from people of all income levels to encompass people of both genders.

Presidents Abraham Lincoln, Ronald Reagan and Bill Clinton famously came from poverty or at least lower middle class socio-economic levels. African-American leaders Bill Cosby, Oprah Winfrey and Maya Angelou came from poverty. Jesus of Nazareth was a carpenter's son, and may have been a carpenter himself, practicing a respectable craft that affords a living but rarely leads to significant wealth. Make no mistake, plenty of leaders were born with a silver spoon in their mouths, and plenty come from something in between poverty and wealth, but the range of wealth is so wide among leaders that it's clear that leadership has nothing to do with how much money you bring to Grand Central Station.

3. Leadership Has Nothing to Do with Formal Education

Look at people like B.J. Palmer, who took chiropractic from a small clinic and school to a major profession nationwide. He dropped out of school after eighth grade. He did pretty well in a leadership role.

Bill Gates, billionaire founder of Microsoft, dropped out of Harvard in his junior year to pursue his interest in software and computer programming, which had been a passion since age 13; if the prestigious college degree was so important, he should have stayed! Steve Jobs left Reed College and went on with Steve Wozniak to found Apple Computer, and likewise made himself very rich. These men, without degrees, transformed society by bringing personal computers into homes and offices everywhere.

You can lead a horse to water, but you can't make him drink. You can send a fool to college, but you can't make him think. . . . Food for thought.

DR. JOHN

John Malone's book titled *It Doesn't Take a Rocket Scientist* tells the stories of "the mavericks, misfits and unschooled investigators who have been responsible for some of the greatest scientific discoveries in history."

Many modern leaders who had university training were mediocre students: Gandhi was said to be a mediocre student and barely passed the admission exam for college in India. He managed to study law in England and pass the bar there but couldn't find a job as a lawyer in India and was even turned down for a job teaching school. Einstein got a degree in science, but along the way he was considered a mediocre student.

Sure, plenty of leaders have had private tutors and advanced degrees, but their ranks are no more likely to yield leaders than those with GEDs instead of high school diplomas or pass-fail reports from the school of hard knocks. Being a college standout or a dropout does not determine your aptitude for leadership or your ability to make your vision become reality.

It's not what you know; it's what you do with it that counts. Or, as New Orleans blues man Dr. John sings in "Qualified": "Yo edgemacashun ain't no hipper than what you understand."

If leadership doesn't have anything to do with who you know, how much money you have, or how much formal education you have, what is it then?

"Vision is the Commodity of Leaders . . ."

Most people in business and in society in general consider Lee Iacocca to be a leader in our society. He rebuilt the failing Chrysler Corporation and reestablished the fading American auto industry. (Of course, since then American car companies find themselves struggling again and readjusting to a global economy.) But in his day, Iacocca— whether or not you liked his style—demonstrated real leadership. Very few people even remember that, while still at Ford, Iacocca was responsible for the wildly successful Mustang and was a force behind the development of the Pinto. As president of Ford Motor Co. and presiding over a $2-billion profit for the year, he nevertheless clashed with Henry Ford II and was fired in 1978. He was quickly recruited as Chairman by Chrysler Corp., which was on the verge of going out of business. He is still considered to be one of the phenomenal leaders in our country, maybe even in the world. How come?

Bennis and Nanus said, "Vision is the commodity of leaders. Power is their currency." The difference between Iacocca and others in his industry was the vision he brought to the table. Iacocca went to the United States government to get a guarantee on loans of millions and millions of dollars to save Chrysler. In a capitalistic society, government's role is not to back loans to private business. But Iacocca went to Washington to communicate his vision to Congress.

Chrysler was in deep trouble. The unions were out of control. The Japanese were beating us at quality control. The steel mills had already closed down. The rubber plants were gone and the car industry was on the way overseas. So here goes Lee Iacocca to the United States government to get Congress's backing. And, what did he have when he went to the table? His vision and his ability to communicate that vision. He painted a dire picture of the nation without Chrysler, and he gave them a vision of a nation with a reorganized Chrysler. Congress compared the two and voted yes. Vision is the commodity of leaders. It's the thing that leaders have that everyone else doesn't.

People who have vision will create what they need, even if it doesn't exist and even if people put barriers in front of them.

What does this mean to you and me? What kind of vision do you have for your life personally? What kind of vision do you have in your relationship with your spouse? Most of us don't have visions about our relationship with our spouse. Instead we have the idea that they're going to be there when we get home. We think, Gosh, I hope they're in a good mood today. Those thoughts are not vision. Vision sees possibilities in the relationship, possibilities you can make happen if you live at 100 percent. One of the most powerful possibilities for your relationship with your spouse is that the two of you share a vision. What better way to begin than sharing a vision for raising your children?

If you want to be a great parent, instill in your children a vision or a desire for a vision so that they will arrive in Grand Central Station knowing what track they are heading for, even though aware that vision can change. As parents we certainly need some good management skills like getting our children to school on time, making sure they're clothed, that they get their homework done, and that they have the resources to study with. But I contend you can have all that and, if there's no vision, they're not going to live at 100 percent. In fact, I believe that if you instill the vision, even if you don't provide those resources and management skills, they will somehow figure out how to get them anyway.

What kind of vision do you hold for your career or for your profession? Are you going to stick with the old paradigms? What kind of vision do you hold for your life? Are you going to lean that extra inch and live at 100 percent? What kind of vision do you hold for the world?

It's hard to lead a cavalry charge if you think you look funny on a horse.

ADLAI STEVENSON

A lot of great people are out there, like Millard and Linda Fuller, who founded Habitat for Humanity International in 1976 because they had a vision of affordable housing for lower income people. They had a vision that those people would participate in the labor and pass on opportunity to others. Habitat has built and rehabilitated more than 150,000 houses with families in need, becoming a true world leader in addressing the issues of poverty housing. You can contribute money or labor in concert with Habitat, if housing for the working poor is your vision.

There are people out there who start up foster-parent programs and people who envision a basic education for all children from Third World countries. You can partner in their vision. For 22 bucks a month, you can be a foster parent and clothe, house and educate some of these kids. When I had my own business, our office had some foster kids. The first dollars from our business every month went to them as well as into supporting a world hunger project.

What kind of vision do you hold for the world and how do you see your business fitting into that? If you can't quickly answer those questions, maybe the first step in making your life extraordinary is sitting down and determining what your vision in these areas is going to be.

Giving an individual or organization an image of themselves that's bigger than the one they hold on their own: That's how Bennis and Nanus define leadership. You hold a vision for your relationship, your children, your profession and the world that's bigger than what they hold on their own, and then you begin to make it become a reality.

When our president said we were going to put a man on the moon in the next decade, he gave us a vision of ourselves that was far bigger than the one we held ourselves. And then everyone pitched in to live up to the new vision.

Walt Disney used to have a sign on the way saying, "Make people big." Once he described to his employees a new project they all could work towards. When he finished talking, the story goes, a blue-collar worker in the group said, "I didn't understand much of what you said, but I'll move the dirt real good." He'd signed on to be a part of a winning project because Disney had given him the image of a winner.

"... And Power Is Their Currency"

Iacocca's success at leading Chrysler throughout the 1980s amply illustrates his vision and equally well the second part of the Bennis and Nanus formula for leadership—"Vision is the commodity of leaders, and power is their currency."

Very few people have experienced that currency or have much of it, so I'd like to define the term "power." Power is the ability to translate your intentions into reality. In other words, power is the ability to do what you say you're going to do. Lee Iacocca went to the government with his vision for Chrysler, and the U.S. auto industry, and Congress guaranteed the necessary loans. He then went on television that night and said, I'm going to pay the money back and I'm going to pay it back in less than five years. Everybody roared with laughter because they knew we were never going to see that money again, ever. And then for him to say he was going to pay it back in less than five years—did he take us for fools? But Lee Iacocca did pay all the money back, and he did pay it back in less than five years, in three-and-a-half years, to be exact. Iacocca did what he said he was going to do in a relatively short period of time. Therefore, we can say he's powerful. How come? The only reason is: He did what he said he was going to do and at a high rate of speed. He changed his intention into reality.

Some people are more powerful than others, and the difference is how fast they can change their intentions into reality. For example, some people who come to my seminars go home and, within 24 hours, they've made changes and their new life is up and rolling. Other people come back a year later and they still haven't gotten it started. The difference is how much power they have.

John Kotter writes about key skills in exercising leadership in the classic Harvard Business book entitled *What Leaders Really Do*. Here, in my words, are Kotter's eight:

1. *Have and articulate a vision of something bigger and better than what is.*

2. *Create a sense of urgency about realizing the vision.*

3. *Impart the vision to others, which means saying it early and often.*

4. *Create and sustain a guiding coalition of those who support the vision.*

5. *Remove obstacles to the implementation of the vision.*

6. *Plan for short-term wins.*

7. *Don't declare victory too soon.*

8. *Anchor changes in the culture.*

When you see what Kotter lays out, you realize that leadership is not the mystical thing so many assume. It doesn't depend on charisma. As the Chinese philosopher Lao Tzu put it: "A leader is best when people barely know he exists, not so good when people obey and acclaim him, worse when they despise him.... But of a good leader who talks little when his work is done, his aim fulfilled, they will say, 'We did it ourselves.'"

Leadership is possible for any of us once we acquire the skills and can support our vision. What's more, you don't have to lead a revolution or a Fortune 500 company to be a leader. You can be, you must be, one with your spouse or your children to have extraordinary relationships.

One of the first steps with regard to spreading your vision is talking and writing about it. Yes, saying something is so can make it so. Read on.

*Bennis, Warren and Nanus, Burt (1985). *Leaders: The Strategies for Taking Charge*. New York: Harper & Row.

FACTS ABOUT LEADERSHIP

- Leaders, contrary to what many believe, are made not born. Guess what. You can be one of them. There are skills you can acquire.

- Having a unique vision—for your career, your relationships, your community—is the starting place in becoming a leader. The second half of the equation is transmitting that vision to others, giving them a bigger vision than they would otherwise see.

- Power is the ability to translate the vision into reality with reasonable quickness. The skills needed include creating a sense of urgency, forming a guiding coalition and anchoring the change in the culture.

*My psychiatrist told
me I'm going crazy. I told
him, "If you don't mind, I'd like
a second opinion." He said,
"All right. You're ugly too!"*
RODNEY DANGERFIELD

CHAPTER SEVEN

Surprise!
Saying So Can Make It So

Words have extraordinary power to shift a paradigm, but they have to do more than just stay in your head or even your heart.

HOW DOES A PARADIGM CHANGE? SOMEBODY SAYS SO. "Saying so" has power. "Saying so" can change the world. "Saying so" requires words.

When dozens of commuters go into Grand Central Station headed for White Plains, and the voice on the loud speaker says the 7:21 train has been delayed till 8 p.m. and switched to track C, those dozens of people slow their steps, pause, turn and head in another direction. Because someone said so. And every person they encounter is a different person from the one he or she would have been. In small but significant ways, the world is changed by a few words.

The Gospel of St. John begins: "In the beginning was the Word, and the Word was with God, and the Word was God." While the thrust of that scripture has to do with the role of the Son of God as God's spokesman, in a general sense the text helps us appreciate the potential of power and nobility in a word. Words build up, and words tear down. Words empower, and words diminish. Words validate, and words deny. Words lie, and words tell the truth. Words set boundaries, and words remove barriers. Words give, and words take away. For better or for worse.

Let me remind you that Adolf Hitler may never have taken up a gun and killed, but his words killed an estimated 11 million people. On the other hand, President Ronald Reagan's words, "Mr. Gorbachev, tear down this wall," empowered hundreds of students to start taking the Berlin Wall down piece by piece.

The nation was persuaded and empowered by the words, "I have a dream...." We don't even have to finish the sentence. Dr. Martin Luther King, Jr.'s words are ringing in our ears. The impact was stronger and spread further than his deeds without the words. The ground has been broken for the construction of a monument a few hundred yards from the Lincoln Memorial where in March 1963 King stood on the steps and delivered the dream speech.

King's dream was his vision. What is yours? Until we say so, until we give words to our goal, it is weak and powerless. With words, we can alter people's view of us or of themselves or of the world. We can empower them to pursue their dream or we can discourage them. Or we can persuade them to participate in our vision.

Diminishing a Great Idea

Words can diminish as well as empower. Here's an everyday example of words that discourage by diminishing the power of the speaker and of his audience both. "It's a great idea but...."

"It's a great idea, but management will never go along." "It's a great idea, but our customers don't like change." "It's a great idea, but it's too complicated." "It's a great idea, but it's too simple." And of course, "It's a great idea, but it costs too much."

"It's a great idea but..." means you shouldn't or can't make your great idea into reality and making your great idea into reality is the very definition of power. "But" negates "it's a great idea." "But" says you are powerless. That's what the word "but" is for—to diminish the idea that came before.

"It's a great idea but…" is the least supportive thing a person could say. On the face of it, "You're crazy" sounds even less supportive, but "you're crazy" alerts you that the detractor is extreme, judgmental and maybe hostile, and so you take him less seriously. "It's a great idea but…" is less supportive because it starts out sounding helpful, but it turns negative and more subtly undermines the confidence of the person with the great idea. You have to have twice as much courage to continue as you did before you heard the "but."

"It's a great idea but…" diminishes the possibilities of the person with the great idea. And what it does to the person who says "but" is no better.

Doctors of chiropractic have heard it: "It's a great idea, but I can't come three times a week." The same patient plays golf three times a week. "It's a great idea, but I can't afford it." The same guy is shopping around for a second big screen TV for his house.

You're stuck at home waiting for the cable repairman. Your spouse says, "I have an idea. Why don't you use the time to telephone your mother? Design a tree house with your son? Start that book you're always saying you're going to write?" And you say, "It's a great idea, but…I have too much to do."

It's either a great idea or it's not a great idea; it's not "a great idea but." We use that "but" because then we don't have to be responsible for our own actions. Then we get to live in the realm of "gosh, I'm a really good person because I recognize it's a good idea, but there are just too many obstacles in the way to get it done." So I'm writing to tell you it's either a great idea or it's not a great idea; it's not "a great idea but." The good-idea-but people, and there are a lot of them, are walking around living in the gray world of zero their entire lifetime and never taking responsibility for their lives and actions. They do it with that little word "but" and all the excuses that follow so easily from that little word.

The Three Most Powerful Words

The words "I love you" have been called the most powerful words in the world, and even these words can be used for better or for worse. There's an old song from the 50s, where a guy admits he took a girl out and "I told her I loved her but oh how I lied. . . ." And the refrain says, "Millions of hearts have been broken just because these words were spoken. . . ."

Millions more hearts have been heavy because they have never heard or never spoken these three words. Spoken in truth, they make, enrich and even save relationships.

Remembering Parents' Words

Parenting is the highest form of leadership. The words you say to your children can have a huge and lasting power, far beyond your understanding at the time, whether they were positive or negative words. Look back at what your parents said to you, those words that you repeat often to yourself as an adult because they had so much power—and still do.

My collaborator Letitia remembers the lift she got from some words her father once said to her admiringly, when she was about 14. After explaining something complicated to her, she responded with comprehension and well-reasoned follow-up, and her father said to her, "You'd make a good lawyer." For a while, she took his words literally and wondered if indeed she should become a lawyer. This was in the days when relatively few women did go into law. Her interest in becoming a lawyer faded, but the boost in confidence her father's statement gave her did not. The fact that she even remembers the words shows the impact on her. She's still convinced she'd make a good lawyer even though she chose not to.

Unfortunately, Letitia carries with her also the indelible imprint of her father's words on another occasion when she was about nine. She was supposed to take a roast out of the oven at a certain hour, and she'd gone out to play and forgotten about the roast.

The Words of the Wise prod us to live well. They are like nails hammered home, holding life together.

ECCLESIASTES 12:11

When her father returned, angry about the over-cooked meal, he exclaimed, "What makes you think you're so goddamn special?"

Even without his words, she felt worried and ashamed about the roast. Moreover, she didn't see the relevance of his remark to her failure to take the roast out of the oven. That perceived lack of relevance made the remark seem to come from a more general feeling he had about her, and she took it to heart. Whenever she aspired to something that maybe she couldn't have, she felt guilty. Why do you think you're so goddamn special? She'd hear the words forever. Any daring endeavor she might attempt in her life became a battleground between making "a good lawyer" and thinking she was so goddamn special she didn't deserve success.

I like to think I have used powerful words with my own children from time to time that helped them create the vision to live extraordinary lives. Vision expressed through the power of words can give an individual or an organization an image of itself that is better than the image it carries on its own. I remember with pleasure one occasion where I communicated a new vision to my daughter, Vanessa, who is now a chiropractor in Colorado Springs. I still remember her first day coming home from first grade. She brought home a big piece of paper with finger paints all over it. I noticed scribbled down at the bottom of the page was her name. I knew instantaneously what the teacher had done that day. She wanted to teach them how to write their name, a skill they were going to need for the rest of their lives. She wanted to make it fun and interesting for them so she had them do finger paintings and then sign their art at the end of the day.

So here came Vanessa with a piece of paper almost as big as she was. When she walked in the house, I was on the telephone and she was standing there with just her eyes beaming over the top of the page, waiting for me to get off the phone. I saw how important this occasion was to her, so I got off the phone and I regaled her with everything I know about art, which took me only two minutes. I made a big deal about her painting. I talked about perspective. I talked about primary colors, about how she mixed them. I used words like "intersection," "vibrant," and "mosaics of secondary colors." I talked about depth perception and contrast. I said: "I didn't know you were an artist! How could you live with me for six years, and you never told me you had this talent?"

I got on the telephone and called up her granddad and explained all this to him. Vanessa just stood there. She had no idea what was going on; she just knew she had done something good. That evening she went upstairs and made dozens of pictures for me. She brought them in and presented them to me folded up with paperclips and I opened them up like the grand opening of an art gallery. She presented them to me as if they were masterpieces. I said wonderful things about them, and she would go back and make another one.

Today she is a fabulous artist. She does portraits in fine pencil. If you stand back even a few feet from one of her drawings, it looks like a photograph. She is extraordinary.

On Vanessa's first day home from school, I could have ignored her pictures and stayed on the telephone. But I showed up in Grand Central Station aware and knowing where I was headed. In that moment, I gave her an image of herself as an artist that was much bigger than the image she held of herself on her own. That's called vision. And I conveyed it in words.

Remembering the Words of Siblings

The cover story of the July 10, 2006, *Time* magazine describes findings of researchers who describe the importance of siblings in making us who we are. We spend more time with our siblings than we do with our parents or our peers, and they are typically the longest lasting relationships of our lives. The words of siblings can work wonders or cause wounds.

Years ago, on the way home from Norway where I'd spoken to the chiropractic association there, I decided to stop by Berlin to see the Berlin Wall. I had Vanessa with me, then 10 years old. She'd traveled seven times around the world with me, going to the Valley of the Tombs in the middle of the Egyptian desert and to the Taj Mahal in India, but, of all the places in the world that she's been, I believe that no place impacted her more than the Berlin Wall. The reason I know is that she went home and told her five-year-old sister Alexis about going into Berlin through military check points. Ever afterwards, Alexis wouldn't go to East Berlin or even to the Wall when we went to Europe. Every time we put Berlin on the itinerary, she refused to go. I found out later that the reason why she wouldn't go was she was afraid that, if we went there, we might not be able to get out. I have no idea what Vanessa told her, but I know her words must have been incredibly powerful. Children can put the fear of God into their siblings with words.

Remembering Teachers' Words

Look back at the things your teachers said to you. I remember a teacher in sixth grade who didn't like me much. Once I had to get up and talk about something in front of the whole class. I did it with ease and thought I'd done a great job. As I was walking back to my seat, the teachers said something embarrassing about my presentation, and all the students' eyes followed me to my seat. I promised myself at that moment that I would never, ever again stand up in front of a group and present my ideas. And I didn't until I was 25 years old.

Letitia remembers many good things teachers said to her about her work because she was a good student. Words that stand out as making a difference, however, came from a different area of school. Her gym teacher was supervising a routine basketball practice, not of the varsity, not of the junior varsity, but of a gym class. Letitia, an average player, remembers being quick but not particularly skilled with the ball. One day, she made three baskets in a 20-minute period, her all-time high. At the end of class, the gym teacher, said, "See you tomorrow, Hot Shot." Hot Shot? It didn't matter that Letitia knew she was an average player, knew that tomorrow she'd probably not make any baskets at all. She'd been Hot Shot for a day. She says she'll never forget the feeling—not about making three baskets but about being called "Hot Shot" once in her life. See, you don't forget words that empower, just as you don't forget words that diminish. You can make or break a child's confidence in a couple words.

Remembering the Words of Strangers

Letitia remembers a stranger's words that lifted her at a time when she was on the threshold of change. She was alone at a convention in another city. A tour bus took participants to a show in a tourist area. There was rousing music and good cheer, and people who came with friends were having a lot of fun. Letitia was feeling a bit lonely, but she made a point of doing a little bit of soft shoe to the music, the only dance steps she knew, all by herself. She was reticent about doing this, but she forced herself to pretend she was having a ball.

Words have the power to both destroy and heal. When words are both true and kind, they can change our world.

BUDDHA

The Master of Ceremonies at one point in the evening chose people from the audience to lead a parade around the room. The emcee chose her, presumably, because she seemed willing to perform in public. He gave her a baton and sent her off. Leading a parade was well out of Letitia's comfort zone, but she knew she couldn't walk around the room as sedately as if she were leading the high school graduation processional; she knew she had to pretend again. So she forced herself—and this was hard—to do an imitation of drum major moves she'd seen in movies or on TV. She felt like she was making a fool of herself, but she forced a smile as she held the baton high and pranced to the beat. When the emcee took the baton, she was both pleased she'd pushed herself and relieved her performance was over.

As the group re-boarded the bus, a man said to her, "You've got some great steps. You are the most confident person I've ever seen!" These words rocked! What they said to her was not that she had great confidence—she knew that wasn't true—but these words validated her dictum "fake it till you make it." Today, when she has to move forward with a confidence she doesn't feel, she looks in the mirror and says to herself, "You've got some great steps. You are the most confident person I've ever seen, Hot Shot."

The moral of the story is, when you're thinking something uplifting, don't just think it, say it. The more specific, the better. You never know when your remark will become a guiding light in someone's life. When you're thinking of something belittling, keep it to yourself. Ask yourself instead, what's something good I could say sincerely at this moment? Those substitute words may not go down in history, but at least the negative words you might have said will not be emblazoned on anyone's psyche to their detriment—and yours.

Changing the Larger World with Words

A lot of people have had a lot of great ideas, but until they put them into words, they had no impact. We can't change a paradigm with thoughts that stay inside our heads. A lot of people have had great ideas and said them to a few people. Maybe those few people's lives were changed, but maybe they didn't repeat the words and not very many people heard them. Getting the words out to as many people as possible is how great ideas change old paradigms in the larger world.

You change your own personal paradigm, the way you look at some aspect of your world, by saying so. You change the paradigm for a lot of people if you send your words out into the world. The further you can send them the more you change the world. It may be by word of mouth or by a seminar or by a pamphlet you give to your customers.

Thomas Paine, who promoted many of the ideas that appeared in the Declaration of Independence, was known as a pamphleteer. He got the word out by pamphlet because publishing a book was very expensive—and still is. His words and the more tempered but still radical words of people like Benjamin Franklin and Thomas Jefferson were combined in the Declaration of Independence, surely one of the most influential documents in history, one that put vision down on paper to give it the power to become reality. In more ways than one, the creation of this document was a revolutionary act; the vision expressed in it created a war; the power to make the vision a reality created a nation.

As a leader, you need to get your words out by going beyond your comfort zone and stretching to meet new audiences that might frighten you a bit. Through practice, you will grow in your ability to make your words public.

The Decision to Speak Out

I remember when it first dawned on me that I needed to speak publicly about what I'd been saying to patients one on one, that I needed to break my vow never to speak in public, and I remember how little prepared I was to face an audience. I'd been telling individual patients about chiropractic, about how their bodies worked, and about what adjustments accomplish. At first, I'd talk about eight minutes to each patient; then as I got more eloquent, I talked for about 18 minutes. Sometimes I was running up to a half hour. When I finished the day, I'd been talking for hours and saying pretty much the same thing over and over. So my partner, Ciro Rustici, said we'd have to start doing health care classes, which are talks about chiropractic, to groups of patients on a weekly basis instead of giving the same message to individual patients every day. He was right, but I was terrified.

I planned my talk for 12 weeks. I made charts, I wrote outlines, I made notes to put on the back wall to remind me of what I was supposed to say, and I stayed late at night practicing. Ciro was doing none of this. He said to just say the same thing that we always said to every patient one on one. It would come easily, he said, because I was so practiced that I explained the topic automatically, without really thinking about it. I agreed with him, but I went back to planning and practicing.

The first night of our talks, Ciro spoke first because it was so easy for him. He got up there in his 1974 John Travolta, Saturday Night Fever polyester pants, his fake-silk shirt and his white patent leather belt. He was looking good. He had agreed to use one of my charts, and he was all set to go. "Good evening, I'm Dr. Rustici," he said. "I'm a doctor of chiropractic." Then for 10 seconds he stood there silent. I started timing him. He stood there for 30 seconds, a minute, a minute and a half. Nothing was coming out of his mouth. Nothing was going on in his brain either, but the audience didn't know it. They thought the silence was high drama. I heard a woman nudge her husband and say, "Damn, he's good." The audience knew that what was going to come out of his mouth next was going to save their lives.

Then there was a moment when I could see Ciro was going to recover. He began to move his hands and lick his lips and come to life. This was all happening in slow motion for me because I was going to be in his position the next night.

The next thing he did, which is what a lot of amateur speakers do when they're nervous, was jam his hands into his pockets. This has the unfortunate effect, at least it did in 1974, of pulling on the zipper, which unfortunately was unzipped, revealing his peach-colored bikini underwear. I found out the next day that he had panicked the day of the talk and begun to cram from the Toastmasters handbook, which gives 20 tips about preparing for a talk. Number 7 was to go to the bathroom right before the speech. Unfortunately, number 8 wasn't to zip up your zipper. And so I watched in horror as he talked animatedly for 45 minutes. When he realized belatedly what kind of a display he'd made of himself, he was mortified beyond words. But he got up the next week and spoke again, and the week after, and he's been doing it for 35 years. On the other hand, I was so traumatized by the spectacle that it took me another year and a half before I would stand in front of an audience.

Finally, after watching words give power to the vision of those around me and to the great leaders of the world, I decided I wanted my vision to become reality also, and I committed myself to speak in public, on film and video, and finally in print.

Everywhere I look, I notice people who have made the decision to speak out, people who were not given pulpits and press releases and asked to speak but people who had a vision and made the difficult decision to put their vision into words and make the effort to bring it to the attention of the public.

For example, Alex Ledesma-Lacson, a modest lawyer in the Philippines, became a leader by writing a book entitled *12 Little Things Every Filipino Can Do to Help Our Country*. It's a book about citizenship and how to live an extraordinary life in the service of his country. It's a simple little book that tells people to follow traffic laws, not to litter, to recycle, and to say positive things about their country. To everyone who buys his book he says, "Help me spread its message." Many thousands of copies of the book have been sold mostly by word of mouth.

Ledesma-Lacson explains, "The book, in many ways, has made

me the kind of person I have always wanted to become—a book author, an ambassador of my Creator, and a patriot of my country. I want my children to remember and say someday that their father loved God and his country so much, and I want them to do the same." He has become his vision through the power of words.

I saw an example of the power of words recently in a school bulletin board display about 20 great women scientists. I'd never heard of any of them. Scientists don't get a whole of popular attention.

These scientists had published in professional journals, but mostly their vision was not expressed where the public would be aware of it. They didn't use the power of words to its fullest extent. But in this display there was one scientist, Helen Sawyer Hogg, whose most important research was on "variable stars in globular clusters." Now I don't know a globular cluster from a chocolate pecan cluster, but she wrote about a hundred scientific papers on the subject. Few people outside of astronomy know that. But hundreds of thousands of ordinary people know more about astronomy than they would have because she wrote an astronomy column in the *Toronto Star* from 1951 through 1981, sharing her vision of the importance of the stars with that newspaper's readers. She also wrote a book called *The Stars Belong to Everyone,* and she hosted a TV series about astronomy in the 1970s. They don't keep a columnist in the newspaper or a show on TV if nobody reads or watches it, and Helen Hogg was in the public eye for over 30 years. This one woman turned people on to astronomy and made more people aware of the stars than the other most accomplished astronomers in modern history, whoever they are because I don't

Words are the most powerful thing in the universe. . . . Words are containers. They contain faith, or fear, and they produce after their kind.

CHARLES CAPPS

know their names. That's the power of words.

Carl Sagan took up where Hogg left off by doing much the same thing for an even larger audience. The noted astronomer, a Cornell University professor, devoted his professional life to searching for intelligent life in the universe and investigating the origin of life on earth. With his storytelling gift, he brought in huge audiences to his 13-part PBS series "Cosmos," which probably reached more people than his eight books. He made science accessible and attractive to the public. Twenty-five years later his "Cosmos," first aired in 1980, was presented again on The Science Channel.

Arguably, science more than anything is responsible for the quality of our lives in the modern world, and yet too few people pursue studies in science to meet the needs of our society. Those who do were probably turned on by those few scientists who used the power of words to express their vision.

Here's another person who saw a possibility few had seen before; he wanted that possibility to be real, so he said so. His name is Jack Williams, and he had the idea that children living in foster care who were unadoptable because of physical, emotional or mental difficulties were actually—guess what?—adoptable! He believed strongly that every child deserves a loving and supportive home no matter what. And he said so.

He went to the Massachusetts Department of Social Services and the Massachusetts Adoption Exchange and told them his new paradigm: Together we can get these unadoptable children adopted. Jack Williams was a very popular news anchorman in Boston, so not only did he have the power of words but he had the Power of Words at his disposal. He told the management of his station (then WBZ-TV4, now CBS4) what he wanted to do. Every Wednesday he'd spotlight one special needs child in a segment called "Wednesday's child." He'd write and edit on his own time if the station would run it. He never chose the child; he let the agency do that. He took the child and his production crew to a place chosen according to the child's interest and engaged him or her (more of them are boys) so the audience could see and hear the child interacting. They went to the fire station, the zoo, or the mall, wherever the child felt the most relaxed. He interviewed the child a bit about his interests, his grades, and his hopes. He'd ask a boy, "What kind of guy are you?" He let the boy tell viewers what he wanted in his life. Every Wednesday, the children said they wanted a place they'd never have to leave, they wanted a loving family, siblings, a dog, a home. See, these kids also have the power of words to change their lives, if someone will just give them an outlet. Out of more than 850 editions of "Wednesday's Child" over 525 special needs children have found adoptive families. The concept has spread to other cities. Change the paradigm, then change the world—with words.

Keeping Your Word

Because words have so much power, it's important not to say them carelessly. Keeping your word, even a promise lightly spoken to a child, especially to a child, is more important than we may realize. A man told me how he never forgot a visit to Salt Lake City, Utah. He and his family went to hear the Mormon Tabernacle Choir sing, where he was awed by the organ. His father told him that after the concert he would take him into the back of the concert hall behind the scenes and show him the organ pipes. After the concert, the boy waited for this to happen. However, they looked around, bought some ice cream, and left without having seen the organ pipes. The boy's disappointment was keen, and he tells the story every now and then, keeping it alive in his consciousness. Even now he operates from the paradigm of not-having-seen-the-promised-organ-pipes. He views his father as author of this paradigm; he still wonders why his father didn't keep his word.

Not keeping one's word is a common parental failing, but it doesn't have to be. A parent just has to be *aware* of what he is saying and of the power of his words.

My collaborator Letitia told me a story from her childhood in Massachusetts. She remembers, the year she was nine, being very attracted to the shape of a scallop shell, the one depicted on the Shell Oil signs. She'd seen all kinds of common clams and mussels but nothing quite so elegant as the scallop. Her great aunt, with whom she spent her summers, said one day that there were a lot of these shells on Cape Cod and remarked, "We'll drive down to Cape Cod and see them some time this summer." This image of scampering along the beach, picking up scallop shells was powerful. However, as the weeks passed, the little girl saw no sign of plans for the trip. Worried that it wouldn't happen, she reminded her great aunt. "When are we going to Cape Cod to find the scallop shells?" The aunt had suggested the trip just as conversation and with only a vague intention of following through. She thought the idea would soon be forgotten. But children don't forget our word. The great aunt was *aware* that her credibility was on the line and that her integrity was tested. Not wanting to make the trip, which would take the better part of two days and involve an overnight stay, she said, "I'll tell you what. You can choose between a trip to Cape Cod and horseback riding lessons." Letitia thought for a few minutes and said, "Horseback riding lessons."

The next week she started lessons, and by the end of the summer could manage a horse and ride to a trot without bouncing. Because she'd loved riding so much, the lessons continued the next year and the year after that until she'd become an accomplished rider, winning ribbons in small horseshows and finally giving riding lessons herself as a summer job during her college years. Letitia's aunt accomplished much of value in honoring her word. Making the trade for the Cape Cod trip was an honest trade and did not go against the promise.

Grown up and on her own, Letitia has at last found beaches where she could collect perfect scallop shells. As a mother herself, she knows how easy it is to say to her children that she will do something with them "some time soon" or "one of these days." She also knows that integrity requires care in promising and keeping her word. Words are powerful.

You might think that, rather than risk having to keep your word, you'll just be quiet about what you're thinking. However, integrity is more demanding than that; integrity often requires you to speak up. Absolute integrity means more than just being a good person. From time to time, you are going to hear someone say something that you know is not right. You may have always kept your mouth shut when you heard this thing being said. You just slipped away because it was not your fight. Integrity requires more. Ayn Rand said that when intellectual revolutionaries who are changing the world hear something said that they know is wrong, they have a powerful weapon in their arsenal. They hold up their hand, they do not argue, and they simply say, "I disagree. You can be an intellectual revolutionary, a paradigm shifter, a leader, if you can say, 'I disagree.'"

If the people who said something wrong are intellectually honest, they will listen to what you have to say and they may change. If not, the next time they say it, you will have undercut their confidence and they are less likely to say it with authority. Their position will have been weakened by your calm and powerful words: I disagree.

Who are you in Grand Central Station? How do you show up? Do you come with your beliefs firm, your values intact, your integrity leading the way, and the words to say so?

WORDS TO LIVE BY

- Don't let the phrase "actions speak louder than words" undercut the value of words. The fact is they change lives and the course of history.

- Remember that words said to you and those you say to others can do extraordinary damage or can lift to the skies. Be careful what you say and write. At the same time, don't hold back when something needs to be said.

- Keeping your word—whether it's with your children or important people in your business contacts—is vital to whether you are viewed as a person of integrity, and, if you are, that fact can pay big dividends down the road.

PROFILE

Lech Walesa

AN ELECTRICIAN WHO REWIRED THE SOVIET WORLD

If you were to pick a handful of people who brought an end to communism in Europe, you'd pick Soviet leader Mikhail Gorbachev, Pope John Paul II and, without doubt, Lech Walesa. He shines as an example of commitment to a cause.

Walesa, the leader of the Solidarity movement, led the Poles out of communism and changed the 20th century. As *Time* magazine pointed out, "It is one of history's great ironies that the nearest thing we have ever seen to a genuine workers' revolution was directed against a so-called workers' state. Poland was again the icebreaker for the rest of Central Europe in the 'velvet revolutions' of 1989."

Born into a family of peasant farmers, Walesa worked as an electrician in the huge shipyards on the Baltic coast. Upset by the repression of shipyard workers in the 1970s, Walesa joined and soon became the leader of the occupation strike at the Lenin Shipyards in Gdansk in 1980. But Walesa was not your average protester. He had the big idea that more was needed for his fellow workers than higher wages; his idea—free trade unions. Surprisingly, the Polish communists conceded, and the movement was christened Solidarity. Soon it had 10 million members, with Walesa at its helm.

Solidarity existed for a while in uneasy tension with the state, then was suppressed by martial law—Walesa spent several months in prison—but Solidarity refused to die. The astute, though erratic politician was ever its symbol, and he was awarded the Nobel Peace Prize in 1983. Walesa joined another occupation strike at the Lenin Shipyard in 1988. A few months later, the Polish communists entered into negotiations with Solidarity, at the first Round Table of 1989. Walesa and his colleagues secured semi-free elections, and Poland suddenly had its first non-communist Prime Minister in more than 40 years. Walesa later was elected Poland's first noncommunist President, a post he held until 1995. Where Poland led, the rest of Central Europe soon followed—and the Soviet Union was not far behind.

Time summed up his contribution this way: "Without Walesa, the occupation strike in the Lenin Shipyard might never have taken off. Without him, Solidarity might never have been born. Without him, it might not have survived martial law and come back triumphantly to negotiate the transition from communism to democracy. And without the Polish icebreaking, Eastern Europe might still be frozen in a Soviet sphere of influence, and the world would be a very different place."

*To work in the world
lovingly means that we are
defining what we will be for,
rather than reacting to
what we are against.*
CHRISTINA BALDWIN

CHAPTER EIGHT

For a Bright Future, Clean Up Your Past

Your feeling powerful begins with making a list of regrets and resents, and then resolving every one.

———————

OWERFUL PEOPLE CAN LIVE EXTRAORDINARY LIVES IN THE present and change the world for the future only if they have completed their past. That means they have settled matters in their past so that they hold no present resentments and regrets and they acknowledge the positive deeds and influences of family, mentors and heroes.

Powerful people are always complete. I went to a seminar long ago where we had to construct what are known as "regret and resent lists." Regrets are things that you have done to other people that you didn't get cleaned up. They may not even know that you did it to them. The insurance company for which the doctor changed the diagnosis just a little bit. That's a regret isn't it? The time you cheated on your spouse. That's a regret. The time you skipped school and didn't tell your parents. The time you told your dad that the car got hit by a careless driver not that you hit somebody and you were at fault. Those are all regrets. Things we have done to other people that we didn't clean up at the time.

"Resents" are things that other people have done to us that didn't get cleaned up. For example, the man who is still perturbed that his father promised to take him to see the organ pipes behind the Mormon Tabernacle Choir and didn't follow through. This man, at only seven years old, didn't call his dad on the broken promise. That kid could have said, "Dad you said we were going to show me the pipes." Clearing this up could have allowed him to spend the next 50 years of his life making things work instead of complaining about his father.

How I know this story is that this man came to several of my seminars. He always came late, and he never took notes as other people often do. Finally, one day he "got it." He raised his hand and told the whole audience about how never a day went by that he didn't remember this slight his father had done to him. He had let the omission grow inside him and made up reasons why his father hadn't kept his word. None of these reasons were that his father simply forgot; they all involved some negative feeling or intent of the uncaring father about the unworthy boy. These made-up explanations made him incapable of living at 100 percent. We took up a collection of change and told the man to call his father and settle this and report back. He made the call and found that his father didn't even remember going to the concert of the Mormon Tabernacle Choir, let alone that he had promised to take the boy to see the organ pipes. It suddenly seemed a silly and sad reason for the man to have been resentful all these years.

So you still resent and blame other people for what they did to you or failed to do. I'm asking you now to construct a list of your regrets and resents. You may well wonder, "How do I know whether it's a big enough matter to go on the list?" Let me tell you something. If you think about it, if it flashes through your mind more than once, it goes on the list because all resents are big. Legally they aren't all big, but how they impacted someone else's life emotionally and what they meant to him or her can certainly be big.

In another seminar where we were doing this work of constructing regret and resent lists, I asked if anyone in the room wanted to share a regret and this young woman in her early 20s said, "When we were about 14 years old, there was an elderly couple who lived next to us and we used to pick strawberries for them because they couldn't pick their strawberry patch any longer. They just took us at our word as to how many little baskets of strawberries we had picked, and they would pay us per basket. We would always cheat two or three baskets and tell them more than what we had actually picked."

No, the world didn't stop because of this incident, but let's see what it means. I said to this young woman, "So you are a what?" She said, "Well, I'm a cheater." I said, "No, you're not." I said, "You're a what?" She said, "I was dishonest." I said, "No, no, no. You're a what?" See we don't even want to say what we really are. I said again, "You're a what?" Do you know that she couldn't even see it or say it. So I asked everyone in the room what was she? They said, "She's a thief. She's a common thief." She robbed money from people, elderly people. Now legally if she had broken in through their window and stolen the money off their counter, she could have gone to a detention home. That's the legal part of it. What's the difference whether she went in through their window and got it or whether she cheated? She is a thief. She calls it cheating so she doesn't have to deal with being sleazy. You know what I'm going to tell you? You and I are all sleazy and we've got it covered up by all this stuff: Well, we cheated; we told a white lie. No, you didn't; you told a big old fat lie. We are all sleazy.

George Bernard Shaw said he had a certain dream every night of his life. He said it was a nightmare that woke him up every single night, sometimes many times. In this nightmare there was a horrible, ugly, distorted being with a face so ugly he couldn't even stand to look at it. That ugly face in this dream came from the distance and stopped right up in front of him so that he had to stare it in the face.

The dream was so frightening that it woke him up every single night. One night he realized he was going to have to confront this thing and see what it was because he couldn't continue like this forever. So one night when the creature came to him in his dream, he deliberately didn't wake up. He stayed there and confronted the being for as long as it took. The face was horrible and he tried to look away but the being wouldn't let him. And Shaw recalled that the longer he looked at it and the closer it got, the worse he felt. All of a sudden he realized that the monster was his life. And he had to take this ugly thing in his arms and hold it. Until we can take our ugly lives in our arms and hold them, we can't go on to fulfill our potential and to live at 100 percent.

Nothing else can quite substitute for a few well chosen, well timed, sincere words of praise. They're absolutely free and worth a fortune.

SAM WALTON

You have to pay for everything. The strawberry thief is going to pay for her theft with her life because the possibilities in her life are now diminished. She wrecked her relationship with those people forever because she can't be comfortable with them again. She wrecked her relationship with her friends that were thieving along with her because they all knew she was a thief. And she thinks less of herself.

Going "Down Front"

Powerful people don't have any more or less misbehavior and dishonesty than anyone else. Here's the difference. Powerful people have completed these processes. Their experiences are still there, but they have completed them.

To live an extraordinary life, you're going to have to find a way of confronting all these ugly things in your life, no matter how big or how small you imagine them to be. How do you confront them? It is very simple though hardly easy. You have to go and complete them with the people who were involved in the process. Here's how you know when they are complete. They are only complete when the other person says they are. You know what that means? You may have to go back to the relationship, the marriage that you were in two decades ago that you're not even in any longer because you're in a new one, and you have to handle the extramarital affairs from that relationship that the other person never even knew about. And you say, "Why bother bringing them up? It's old dead stuff." You know why? Because, if it's in your mind, it's not old dead stuff. And you can't ever have a real relationship with that person, and you can't even have a real relationship with the spouse you're with now until you've got those old issues cleaned up.

Powerful people are always complete. "But," you say, "how do you complete things with people who aren't around any longer or who wouldn't see you? How do you deal with these obstacles?" And no, writing your apology down for yourself isn't good enough. I'm telling you this because some people say, "You just need to forgive yourself." No, you need to perform an act to be forgiven. An act, not a thought. I grew up in a Southern Baptist church, evangelical long before that was ever in vogue. In my little farming community, 100 people on an

Easter Sunday was a good Sunday for us. In the Bible it says in order to be saved you have to believe and have faith. In that little church they had a twist to it. Not only did you have to believe, you had to go down front. You go down to the front of the sanctuary and you say you believe, down front where people can see you and hear you. There is something about the act of going down front that makes it different—harder to do and more life changing.

The 2003 movie *Something's Gotta Give* with Jack Nicholson playing Charlie is a wonderful portrayal of a man who couldn't commit to a healthy love relationship. He was in love with Erica, played by Diane Keaton, but couldn't commit to her. After Erica discovered him with another woman, she got angry and broke up with him and went on with her life. Charlie finally realized what he was missing. But he didn't come running after her. First, he decided that what he needed to do was to become complete. He took off six months to go around and find all the women he had dated and treated poorly and cheated on in the past. Some slammed the door in his face, some introduced him nicely to their new husbands, some walked away without listening to his apologies. When he had finally put all his other misdeeds behind him, he came back to find Erica, knowing it might be too late. He wanted to "go down front" to profess that he had changed. He figured she might take him back, but that, even if she didn't, he could finish his mission of becoming complete. If you haven't seen the movie, I won't tell you the ending. Even if you have seen it, it's worth spending some time watching Charlie make amends and understanding how those acts made it possible for him to live hereafter at 100 percent.

Resentment is like taking poison and waiting for the other person to die.

ANONYMOUS

Completeness on a Grand Scale

The African Reconciliation Movement was an example of completeness for a whole nation. The African National Congress, under the leadership of Nelson Mandela, promoted national reconciliation in South Africa and set up a national unity government, which included the National Party, the party of the white oppressors.

The South African Truth and Reconciliation Commission (TRC) was set up in 1995 as a constitutional body by the Government of National Unity to help deal with what had happened under apartheid. Archbishop Desmond Tutu was Chairman of the Commission based in Cape Town. Both perpetrators and victims were urged to come before the Commission to tell the truth about what they'd done or what they'd suffered. Victims often asked for restitution, often reasonable things like a gravestone for a murdered family member, money for education, or health care. In addition, in the first year of the commission, over 3,500 perpetrators of violence or abuse confessed and asked for amnesty, which was sometimes granted. Many sessions were broadcast on national television, allowing the whole nation to absorb the power of completeness in the form of confessing and making amends. While not all agree the Commission was a success, many see the TRC as a crucial component of the transition to a democracy for all citizens in South Africa.

Personal Truth and Reconciliation

Who have you harmed and how can you become complete with them? If you can't find the person or persons you've wronged, you've got to make restitution. I have a friend who used to steal bikes when he was growing up. He stole over 100 bicycles and sold them. He was at the seminar I've been talking about, and he decided he was going to clean up that regret. He couldn't ever go back and find all those people whose bikes he stole. So over the next two years he went out and, with all of his spare income from his job, he bought 100 bikes and gave them to children in ghetto areas. He figured it was better to pay with bikes than with the rest of his life. You are going to pay one way or another, so you can choose a sincere restitution as close to the type and magnitude of your misdeed as you can. You are paying right now with your life at zero unless you pay up in some other way more beneficial to society and those you've wronged. Norman Cousins said that the tragedy in life is not dying, it's what dies inside of us while we're alive. That's the real tragedy.

How does being incomplete hold you back and becoming complete allow you to move forward to an extraordinary life? I think Mary Manin Morrissey, a New Thought minister and author, said it very well, her words transcending her own personal history.

> *Even though you may want to move forward in your life, you may have one foot on the brakes. In order to be free, we must learn how to let go. Release the hurt. Release the fear. Refuse to entertain your old pain. The energy it takes to hang onto the past is holding you back from a new life. What is it you would let go of today?*

So, you know what I'm going to ask you to do? Clean up your regrets and resents. Begin today. If you just go out and clean up one of them, you'll feel so powerful you'll feel like a new person. Clean up every regret and every resentment, every single one of them—it can take you years to do that—but, if you clean up every single one of them. you know where you will then be? At zero. Being at zero doesn't make you powerful except in comparison to where you probably are now—well below zero. If you can get to zero, you can live in the present. You'll be back to when you started your life decades ago when your possibilities were endless. You can now begin to build an extraordinary life.

There's something to be learned from my collaborator Letitia's story of resentment and regret. She didn't go to any of these seminars I've mentioned, so she was figuring this out on her own a little bit differently. She was aware that for many decades she had harbored resentment towards her mother for favoring her brother, for example, keeping him with her while their father was away in the Navy and sending her away to stay with relatives. This and other slights she turned over in her mind fairly often. She finally asked her mother why she gave her to relatives while her father was away. Her mother said, "Because they wanted you." She asked her mother why, when she came to visit during that time, she never paid any attention to her. Her mother said, "You didn't pay any attention to me, so I didn't pay any attention to you." These answers didn't satisfy Letitia, who felt it was a mother's job to pay attention to her child so she'd know what a mother-child relationship was.

One day, in order to diminish her resentments and work up some more positive feelings, she decided to write down a list of all the good things her mother had done for her over the years and the positive influences she'd had. She especially got to thinking about how it was from her mother that she got her creativity and that her mother had always encouraged her writing and other forms of creative play. Letitia wrote down how her mother had taken her to plays at an early age, and now she writes plays. She remembered how her mother taught her how to memorize poetry and remember French object pronouns easily. She listed all the creative things her mother did, too, like never using store-bought gift-wrap but making decorations herself for every gift. These examples of creativity taught her that originality and creativity were important, a lesson that has served her well. When she finished making the list of her mother's positive acts and influences, she wondered what to do with it. She was trying to think of something symbolic to do with the list when the obvious occurred to her: She could mail it to her mother. Her mother was delighted and said it brought back many pleasant memories of activities she'd forgotten. I'd like to say everything was healed by that deed. It was not, but Letitia enjoyed her mother's pleasure and felt a certain satisfaction about her acknowledgement of her mother's positive gifts. An act of acknowledgement never hurts and often helps, whether you know the outcome or not. Good deeds deserve acknowledgement regardless of the rest of the relationship.

Acknowledging what the good people have done for you in the past is the rest of the process of completing yourself. Your reconciliation with the past is not finished until you tell those to whom you owe much or little that you appreciate what they gave to you.

In my own case, I remember with satisfaction the time I took a big step towards completion by acknowledging my dad's great gifts to my life. My dad came from a generation where they don't talk about love, especially men. Their idea was that you love, but you don't talk about it. In fact, my dad's last birthday party was the most wonderful birthday party I have ever been to in my life, and there was no exchange of gifts or cards or any of that kind of festivity. My dad had never talked about his life. In order to get some of his life story out of him, my mother made up a five-page test for everyone to take at his party. The items on the test were multiple choice, fill in the blanks, true and false, and some essay questions, all about my dad's life and his parents' and his grandparents' lives. It took about half an hour for us to finish the test. Because my dad had to tell us what the correct answers were, he was forced to spend a couple of hours talking about his life. It was wonderful.

On the last page were the essay questions including, "If you could say anything to your father that you wanted to say to him, what would you tell him?" And so for the next half hour or so we got to sit around and tell our dad what he meant to us. It was wonderful for all of us. At the end, he was all choked up. He said, "You know, my father never once told me that he loved me, but we all knew he did." He added, "I was never raised to say that either." And he didn't.

So when I called him up on the telephone on a Sunday not long after that, I was looking for an opening, and he was giving me nothing. He didn't know what was coming, and he didn't help me a bit. And finally I just had to jump in and say, "Dad, I just wanted to tell you how much I love you. And there's more." And I told him the things I wanted to tell him. He just listened to it. Dead silence on that phone. And finally, he said, "Great! Want to talk to your mother?"

To forgive is to set a prisoner free and discover the prisoner was you.

ANONYMOUS

There has been a difference, however. My dad and I have always hugged, but the hugs are different now. You know why? Because the hugs are coming from a place beyond zero. Not having regrets and resents gets you to zero. Making acknowledgments gets you beyond.

Putting into words the love I feel for my dad was important to my completeness. Putting into words the need we all have for completeness is my way of changing the paradigm of how we often behave with our parents—silent appreciation—to a new paradigm of expressing our feelings in words, becoming complete with our past and staying complete by saying so.

I felt my vision was validated when, after one of my seminars, I got this letter from a colleague in chiropractic from White Rock, British Columbia:

My dad was recently diagnosed with cancer. . . . I've had to show a lot of strength to help my parents through this. I must admit I've always had my parents there, and I've taken that for granted.

The morning my father went in for surgery I told him for the first time that I loved him. (It had everything to do with what you've taught me, Guy) . . . and you were right . . . the conversations and hugs are different. . . .

Besides Acknowledging Parents, Remember Teachers and Mentors

Acknowledge those that gave your career and your life a boost. Have you ever written to a former teacher about what a difference he or she made to your life? We sometimes find ourselves recalling to a friend or to ourselves a life-changing comment or whole year or semester of support and inspiration. That's the time to pull out a sheet of paper and write this down and drop it in the mail. E-mail will do but paper is better for those who mostly came from the generation of paper and U.S. mail. Do it while you still know how to reach them. Letitia needs to thank that gym teacher for addressing her as "Hot Shot," for example. Actually, that teacher is deceased, so what can she do? Acknowledge another kid, an average player, who has a peak performance you notice on the city courts or at your kid's school. Maybe it's your own kid. Tell him you noticed. Call him "Hot Shot."

There are countless other people who do us favors or boost our confidence. Acknowledge them. Tell them how they changed your life. Do it today.

It's a good idea to keep a box of suitable paper handy for acting on your impulses of gratitude. Remember an act is better than a thought. Make a habit of writing a note a day, acknowledging those who have made a difference to you in the past and those who have helped you today.

This is living at 100 percent, going beyond zero into an extraordinary life.

ADD TO YOUR TO DO LIST

- You can't step into an extraordinary future until you have cleaned up your past. You must resolve the wrongs you've committed against others, and confront and forgive the wrongs done to you.

- If you can't contact the people you need to, perform an act of compensation. If you stole as a child, give things to others today.

- Don't leave things unsaid that ought to be said. For example, do you need to express your love and appreciation for parents, friends, teachers, mentors and others?

MAKE YOUR LIFE EX

CHAPTER   TITLE

9   **LOAD, FIRE, AIM, THEN RE-**

:: FEAR ITSELF

:: THE VISION MUST SURPASS THE RISK

:: ORDINARY PEOPLE, EXTRAORDINARY V

:: START A MOVEMENT

: LOAD, FIRE, AND THEN AIM

Just do it.

NIKE SLOGAN

CHAPTER NINE

Load, Fire, Aim, Then Re-aim

To fly into an extraordinary life, you'll have to walk
to the edge and leap into the unknown.

P OWERFUL PEOPLE, PEOPLE WHO MAKE THEIR VISION INTO
reality, are willing to be at risk in their lives. They are willing
to go forward without knowing the outcome.

In the Bible book of Hebrews, the Apostle Paul writes about
faith. In the translation by Eugene Peterson, this is what you read
about Abraham:

> *By an act of faith, Abraham said yes to God's call to travel to
> an unknown place that would become his home. When he
> left, he had no idea where he was going. By an act of faith he
> lived in the country promised him, lived as a stranger camp-
> ing in tents. Isaac and Jacob did the same, living under the
> same promise. Abraham did it by keeping his eye on an
> unseen city with real, eternal foundations—the City designed
> and built by God.*

Abraham went out with "no idea where he was going." He took
a material risk, that's for sure, leaving a prosperous city to pursue

"the City designed and built by God." But the Bible records that he received unique blessings for his faith. That's what this chapter is about.

There are times when you're forced to make choices and sometimes life-or-death decisions, sometimes very quickly, like choosing which way to swerve when a car is coming straight at you. I've had to make monumental choices of that kind in my personal life and in my career when every option was high risk. In this chapter, I'm not talking about that kind of tough choice you're forced to make; I'm talking about voluntary choice between taking a risk and "getting by," between living an extraordinary life or staying in an old, worn out paradigm because it feels more secure.

Fear Itself

What makes risk so hard? It might turn out badly. Yeah, and it might turn out well. It might turn out bigger and better than you imagined. All the huge successes in the world started out with the possibility, "It might turn out badly." You know what? It might turn out badly anyway. Or worse. In any case, weigh the possible losses with the possible gains. Don't show up in Grand Central Station blind or stupid; be aware, but don't be fearful.

What is fear anyway? Thoughts about possible or impending pain or loss accompanied by adrenaline rush, shakiness, sweating and stammering. You don't die of shaking, sweating or stammering. We sometimes wake up and go, "Uh oh, I'm afraid." Are we going to let that adrenalin stop our whole lives so that we don't go out and do what we know we're supposed to do? Are you going to stand at the pearly gates and when they ask you why you didn't do the right thing you say, "Well, I had some adrenalin running that day." It doesn't sound like much of a defense to me. Forget fear!

Does it make a difference how big the risk is? Of course. Don't take a big risk for a little idea.

Lee Iacocca, when he took over failing Chrysler Corporation, said he was scared to death every time they released a new line of cars. So what. He didn't let those emotions stop him from what he came to do. Chrysler released the line of cars, and people bought them. What if the line had not been popular? The company would have failed. What if he had been too afraid to release the line and there'd been no new models at all? The company would have failed. So what's the difference? None. Putting out a new line of cars was the only action that had the possibility of big success: That is, saving the company, keeping auto workers in business and auto dealers and all the others in the industry. In other words, Iacocca had the emotions; his emotions didn't have him.

The Vision Must Surpass the Risk

Astronauts risk, with every flight, their own lives as well as the nation's hopes; they balance the magnitude of their vision with the size of the risk. They work with people who value excellence as much as they do. Still there is the risk of the unknown.

In 1969, American astronauts took man's first steps on the moon. All the astronauts were risk takers, a breed of fighter pilots and test pilots who had many times faced the unknown. As the first man to step on the moon and the captain of the first moon landing, Neil Armstrong remains the most famous, John Glenn, the first American in orbit, close behind. There's a special place in my admiration, however, for Alan B. Shepard. Playing catch-up with the Russians, the NASA program put Shepard into a suborbital flight in 1961, a small step but, as the first time an American had ridden a rocket into space, it was a morale booster that put us back into the space race. In the movie *The Right Stuff*, someone pointed out derisively that Shepard had little to do but sit there in the capsule while engineers on the ground, who had programmed the flight, manned the controls. A monkey had already done as much, the detractor pointed out. Chuck Yeager, the most celebrated test pilot in the country, countered in Shepard's defense that the monkey hadn't known he was sitting over an explosive charge that would propel him into space with no way of return if anything went wrong. Shepard knew. He was fully aware of the risk he was taking to transform the American space program and to give the American people the confidence to put men into orbit. That meant Shepard was risking 100 percent, and that made his life extraordinary.

Courage is the first of human qualities because it is the quality which guarantees all others.

WINSTON CHURCHILL

Not all risks turn out well, of course. Two manned space flights burned up in flight, and another crew was lost on the launching pad. The risk to turn our vision into reality was a risk of life as well as enormous resources. It had to be a big and worthy vision for such a risk.

In 2006 Atlanta was celebrating the 10th anniversary of the Olympics in this city. The Olympics itself had been a big risk for the city, any city, in terms of money, and the danger of drawing fanatics, foreign and domestic, such as the bomber who actually killed several people and injured many in Olympic Centennial Park. The metro area shared these risks. Moreover, a few individuals took great personal risks in bringing the event to the city. When Atlanta businessman Billy Payne proposed competing for the 1996 Olympics to be held in Atlanta, people mostly thought he was crazy. Payne, however, had a vision and the power to make it become reality. As time went on and his enthusiasm converted doubters, he had a lot of help, but he put his pride and his income at risk for years before he attracted a team that could make it happen.

Payne's risk got even more up close and personal on the day that the winner of the Olympics was announced. It all came down to this one meeting of the International Olympic Committee during which the competitors for the honor of holding the games could do no more than wait. While the committee was meeting to make its decision, Billy Payne began to have chest pains. Maybe it was stress and anxiety. On the other hand, he'd had heart problems before. Most people would have gone directly to a hospital. If he had, the IOC would have immediately learned the news, even as they debated. Realizing that the mastermind of Atlanta's bid was perhaps out of the picture and that Atlanta might not have the same level of leadership to manage the games as they would with Payne at the helm, the IOC would probably have voted for the sentimental favorite Athens, Greece. Billy Payne chose to risk his health and even his life by staying in his hotel suite and waiting out the decision of the Committee before seeking medical help. He had come this far; he wasn't quitting. He'd take the biggest risk of all for his vision. Atlanta won the games; Payne's chest pain soon abated, and he went on to see his Olympic dream come true.

While world-class athletes were training for Olympic trials, many lesser-known people were taking huge personal risks. For example, the firm of Draper & Associates, consultants in program and project management, like many entrepreneurs, offered a great deal of *pro bono* strategic planning for all phases of the big event, in the hopes of winning a contract to make it happen. Before owner and CEO

Gary Draper could see the results, he took a second mortgage on his home to make up for the expense of providing these services. In early 1992, the Atlanta Committee for the Olympic Games (ACOG) contracted with Draper & Associates to provide overall planning and program management services in support of the committee's preparation and delivery of the Centennial Olympic Games. His personal risk paid off in financial success, excitement for all involved, and a contract as consultant for the next Games in Sydney, Australia. The vision for him was worth the risk.

Today's big success is yesterday's big risk.

Ordinary People, Extraordinary Vision

It's not just people with the backing of successful companies who have big vision. Individuals at every level of wealth and income, wanting to live extraordinary lives, take astounding risks to make their vision a reality.

The *Atlanta Journal and Constitution* (August 13, 2006) told the story of Sebri Amir, who, as a teen, with his family's blessing, fled his hometown of Harar, Ethiopia, in order to avoid persecution for his political activities. He walked all the way to the neighboring country of Djibouti. He finally managed to come as a political refugee to the United States where he went to school, raised a family, and built up a business to include several convenience stores and a carwash. These businesses represented security to him. In 2003, in his 40s, he decided to sell one of his stores to open the Yemage Medical Center in Harar, the impoverished city where he was raised. He persuaded the Ministry of Health in Ethiopia to pay for the property, which then secured a loan. He discovered Medshare International in Decatur, Georgia, an organization that collects used and surplus medical supplies to donate to medical facilities in poor areas of the world. He hired doctors and nurses in Ethiopia and bought medical and dental equipment. Fortunately, a dollar goes a long way in Ethiopia, and some of the patients can pay the $7 a day it costs for inpatient care; those who can't pay, the majority of patients, get free care. Amir later sold his carwash to put more money into the hospital. Now he is down to one gas station to support himself and his family here in Georgia. He has sacrificed, and he risks every day for something bigger than he is. He is establishing a foundation to expand his ability to build medical facilities in Ethiopia. He also wants to build a hospice for AIDS patients. He has a vision, and he has taken huge risks to make his vision into reality. Without those risks he would be just another immigrant storeowner getting by.

But wait! What about this man's wife and four children? The Atlanta newspaper published a photo of Sebri Amir and his wife Ashut, who, the paper says, own the Shell gas station together. What about her? She's smiling in the picture, sure, but the article says nothing about her. She's risking, too, perhaps even more than her husband because she may have less to fall back on if their business fails.

Behind every person who takes a big risk, there may be a family taking the same risk or more.

In my own field, Dr. Janice Hughes, a colleague from Canada, disrupted her family and her practice as well as her husband's practice in order to live at 100 percent. "I'd written a life purpose statement," she recalls. "Once while teaching a class about leadership, I realized I was already living my life purpose. The epiphany that came to me was that achieving my life purpose meant that it was time to stretch, to think: What next?" In her practice she could only see a few patients a day, and she had a vision of a broader impact. So she took a big risk.

She closed her very successful practice, uprooted her husband, took her children out of school, left Canada and brought her family to Davenport, Iowa, to help me at the college of chiropractic where I was president. There she did have a wider impact through the education of young chiropractors. Again her vision expanded. At the same time, she wanted to accommodate her husband, who really wanted a hands-on chiropractic practice. "I didn't have to spend a lot of time thinking about it," she says. "It was Boom! And move on." She uprooted her family again and moved to Colorado where her husband could fulfill his vision and she could join The Masters Circle, the largest consulting firm in chiropractic in the world, coaching and teaching chiropractors across the nation about excellence.

"It was a huge risk to leave my country, to take my children out of school and go to a different country to start over," Janice says. "And after a second challenging move, my family and I are now living a wonderful life we could not have imagined before."

Ordinary people, with extraordinary vision, take seemingly small risks that are large in their eyes because of how great the paradigm shift is for them. A teacher I know about volunteered to give a class in creative writing to residents of a group home, children whose families had been torn apart by tragedy. In the class, a boy named Tim wrote about what he'd wish for if a genie gave him three wishes:

"I want to be a cartoonist when I grow up, I mean, to visualize a character in your head and bring it to life is like a wish. You've used your first two wishes that didn't work. But on your last wish instead of letting the genie go, you take a chance and gamble. But this gamble worked. You've gone from a thought process to paper. Then from paper to the screen. Now you're seeing your show or cartoon on live television."

I'm interested in the fact that Tim sees putting a thought process on paper as taking a chance, as a gamble. What is he risking? Very little it seems for most of us. However, writers and artists often experience executing their ideas as risk. Ideas sound so great in our heads and we often fear making them concrete. We've often experienced expressing ourselves and then seeing that our ideas—so grand and fun in our heads—suddenly seem a lot less magical on paper. Somebody says about our vision, "It's a great idea, but...." So we keep it in our heads. Taking what's in our heads and putting it out there for the world to see—that's "saying so." That's a risk.

In many ways, a small risk for one person can be a large risk for someone else. I saw an article in *Simplicity Magazine* (August 2006) entitled "What's the Most Fearless Thing You've Ever Done?" Stories that answered the title question followed. However, most of the deeds described were not *fearless* but *fearful*, accomplished in spite of fear. These actions included physical feats such as ice climbing, dog sledding and cattle herding on horseback. The stories also included emotional challenges such as posing in the nude for an art class, coming out as a lesbian to parents, and throwing a dart on a map and then moving to the place the dart landed in order to start a new life. A couple respondents to the question did a deed for the express purpose of facing their fears. A Utah woman sang our very difficult national anthem *a cappella* at a minor-league baseball game in order to face and overcome her stage fright as a singer. A woman who feared heights shakily made her way on foot across the Capilano Suspension Bridge in Vancouver, 450 feet long and 230 feet above the Capilano River.

> *I am always doing that which I cannot do, in order that I may learn how to do it.*
>
> PABLO PICASSO

All of the people who did these bold deeds were trying to change their paradigm of fear. One said the experience was "frightening, thrilling and empowering." Another said "scary but one of the best moves I've ever made." One woman hit at the heart of the matter when she said, "Now I can do anything."

Like the ropes course I told you about earlier, these bold acts were more about facing fear than about facing danger. The obstacles were scary looking but not really risky. The only risk was confronting fear and saying, "I am no longer afraid." Saying so. The power of words.

The Risk of Being First

Being the first to act from a new paradigm carries special risks. Alan Shepard risked failure to sit on top of a rocket headed for space, just as Neil Armstrong did to be the first to set foot on the moon, but in doing so they had the hopes, prayers, and approval of the American people and millions around the world. How about the people who broke into a new area where only a small minority of people were praying for them and many were hoping for failure? Take Jackie Robinson. Dodgers' general manager Branch Rickey offered Robinson a contract to play ball in the Dodgers organization. Rickey was taking a huge risk to champion a new paradigm: Black people play baseball in the Major Leagues.

However, Robinson himself had to risk a great deal more. Even his life and the lives of his wife and child were threatened by segregationists. Rickey built a strategy to make the move work: being sure Robinson was committed to NOT reacting to slurs, taunts and physical attacks. Then Rickey started him in a Dodgers farm team, the Montreal Royals, because racial prejudice seemed less vitriolic in Canada. He didn't move Robinson to the Brooklyn Dodgers until he was a hero in Montreal. Still the batting titlist's arrival at Ebbets Field in 1949 was hugely risky. Robinson was risking all for himself and his family but also for black people everywhere. His excellence as a player was not the main issue. Holding his temper, acting constantly cheerful instead of sullen, being better than negative stereotypes and bigger than his opponents: These were his challenges. Any slip, and he would have set back the possibilities of his whole people. Robinson ended up with the National League's batting title and was named the League's most valuable player. And he held his temper that whole year. Two men of different races took huge risks to establish a far-reaching paradigm shift: As baseball went, so went American culture. Robinson not only broke the race barrier in sports, he set the stage for the work of Dr. Martin Luther King, Jr.

The first woman, the first Catholic, the first Jew, the first southerner, the first anybody takes big risks to herald a new paradigm of equal opportunity.

When the first woman entered a man's world and achieved prominence, she attracted national attention. The first female Justice of the Supreme Court, the first American woman to serve as a director of a major corporation, the first woman on the President's Cabinet, the first female ordained minister, the first female astronaut, the first woman elected to the Baseball Hall of Fame, and so forth. Still women all over the country must break out of the old paradigm for themselves, again and again, in small arenas in out-of-the-way places.

Unheralded, many ordinary women have taken the risks of facing disapproval and discomfort if not actual opposition by going into career fields dominated by men. I think of a woman named June McNaughton, who married young and had five children with a handsome, charming man who was also a determined alcoholic. When June saw that her husband's drinking was severely undermining their finances and ability to survive, she divorced him. Of course, he had no support to give her.

To dare is
to lose one's
footing momentarily.
To not dare is
to lose oneself.
SOREN KIERKEGAARD

June wasn't afraid of hard work, and she could have taken any number of jobs readily available for women, but she didn't think the salary of those jobs would be enough to raise her children well, so she took a risk. She'd struggle a few more months to feed herself and her children on crumbs in order to prepare herself to make more money in the future in a new industry. She begged neighbors to take care of her children while she took courses in computer programming, a field in its infancy at the time.

She was the only woman in the class. The instructor never looked at her directly or spoke to her. He ignored her completely, even when she raised her hand. She worked hard. Shortly after the class had taken the IBM Programmer Aptitude test, the instructor called her on the phone. He said he had some "very surprising" news for her. He told her she had made the highest score that he had ever seen on the aptitude test. June replied wryly, "And why does that surprise you?" He changed the subject.

She went on to be a system analyst and project manager for several major national and international corporations and raised her children well. Now her grandchildren and great grandchildren turn to her in times of stress, and she has been a mentor to many young people.

Extraordinary people commit to win. They take risks because they expect to win, and they have confidence they will recover from losses.

Just as I admire the women who took risks to be able to do any job they wanted to do, I admire the many courageous black children who integrated the schools in the 1960s, taking enormous physical and emotional risks for the vision of integrated schools and better education for themselves and others of their race. Charlayne Hunter Gault was one of the first two African-American students to enter the University of Georgia. Four decades ago her dignified walk into the University classroom helped make integration of schools a non-issue, a new paradigm. Her willingness to risk derision and even injury elevated her into an extraordinary life. Today, after serving as CNN's bureau chief in Johannesburg, South Africa, for six years, her vision even broader, she has resigned to devote herself to special projects, informing the public on important issues.

Staying in our comfort zones often keeps us from developing a broader vision and making it become a reality. If we never go outside of our comfort zone, which is the paradigm in which we live, that box keeps our life ordinary.

Load, Fire, and Then Aim

Powerful people get things done. Powerless people are paralyzed by analysis; they use the military order of Load, Aim, Fire. Aiming takes up all their time, and they rarely get around to firing. Here's what powerful people do, according to Tom Peters: "Load, Fire and Aim." You know why? Because you are no good at something the first time you do it just like everybody else on this planet. And if you're waiting until you get perfect at it, guess what? You'll never do it. Powerful people load up their ideas and fire them, and then they aim. Now that doesn't mean they're stupid; they just know that, when you're doing something that no one has ever done before or that you yourself have never done before, you don't even know what the questions are, much less what all the answers are. With anything complicated, you have to Load-Fire just to find out what the problems are. Firing is always a risk, but you have to do it to refine your aim. Powerful people Load, Fire, and then Aim, Re-aim and Re-aim for the rest of their lifetimes.

My collaborator Letitia is not only a writer but also a life coach. She loves coaching, but she's uncomfortable promoting herself. She knows that to get the opportunity to live out her vision of supporting people in making positive changes in their lives she must go out of her comfort zone. So she prepared a speech about her coaching, what we call an elevator speech, a message you could give in the time you spend with someone in the elevator. Preparing and memorizing a speech might be considered "loading." She soon discovered that reciting her speech from memory prevented her from being natural and letting her passion for her profession show. So she changed her goal from saying her prepared speech to "just say something." That's firing. She sees what the person fires back and that gives her the information and encouragement to aim.

Letitia has studied risk-taking in several arenas. For example, she writes success stories and other materials for a residential treatment center for young men addicted to drugs and alcohol, Metropolitan Serenity House in Cumming, Georgia, a half-hour northwest of Atlanta. One of the main themes of the success stories and of the whole treatment plan, she says, is that the young addicts take progressively greater risks under the guidance of staff.

Locked-down detoxification units in hospitals can get a drug or alcohol user clean. Treatment centers can keep them clean as long as they keep the doors locked. When they are locked up, they can load but never fire. There is little risk of relapse, while out in the real world the risks for an addict are huge and constant. The only way they can learn to leave the treatment center and stay sober, however, is to take small, well-thought-out risks with the support of the staff. If they succeed, they have increased confidence and knowledge of how to remain sober. If they relapse, they learn from it.

What do other treatment centers do when patients relapse? They kick them out. They get no chance at trial and error. At Serenity House, with the help of the staff, young addicts learn to recognize their triggers for relapse and to redefine the boundaries of safety. Over time, through more risk and more success and/or through more failure and more learning from mistakes, they learn to live sober lives. Without the successive risk-taking they can never learn to live in the real world. Learning to risk, that is, learning to fire without being sure of the outcome is the road to recovery for the addict and to an extraordinary life for the rest of us.

We at Life University are currently developing a "think tank" that will include facilitators for training people in eight values that can and should be applied to national issues like obesity or the need for business that promotes environmental protection. Our name for it, at least for now, is Life Source: The Center for Infinite Thought. It will have eight wings or rooms because of the eight values. How are we going to structure it? What is our plan? We don't know yet. We're going to put it in place—that's loading—then we'll try it out—that's firing—then we'll see how it works and come back and aim. The building and what goes on inside it may someday be something quite different from what we imagine today, but we are building it and staffing it and we'll see where we go later. Load, fire, aim. Even though we don't know exactly how the venture will play out, we believe we can't go wrong because we are always guided by our vision.

Without vision, you cannot have an extraordinary life. Without changing a paradigm from the old to the new vision, you cannot move toward that extraordinary life. Without saying so, you cannot change a paradigm beyond yourself. You must use your power: the power of words, the power of completeness with the past, the power of willingness to take risks to make your vision become a reality and to live an extraordinary life.

LOAD UP WITH THIS

- Sure, taking risks can be scary, but understand that to live an extraordinary life you must realize that overcoming fear is the first obstacle.

- To overcome the fear, the vision must be worth the risk. Concentrate on the possible rewards, get others' encouragement, then go for it. Don't spend a lot of time aiming because you probably won't get it right the first time anyway. Just do it, and then regroup.

- Being the first at anything takes courage, but you truly make your life extraordinary if you can blaze a trail that others will follow. Powerful people expect to win and to recover from losses. That's one reason people follow them.

PROFILE

Nelson Mandela

OVERCOMING APARTHEID, KEEPING INTEGRITY

Nelson Mandela remains an icon of integrity that extends beyond his role as the hero who ended South African apartheid.

He got involved in protests as a college student and later as a lawyer, where he was daily exposed to the inhumanities of apartheid, kindling in him a passion for change. However, according to *Time* magazine, there was little likelihood of a revolution. "The classic conditions for a successful revolution were almost wholly absent: The great mass of have-nots had been humbled into docile collusion, the geographic expanse of the country hampered communication and mobility, and the prospects of a race war were not only unrealistic but also horrendous."

Mandela first opted for passive resistance as a strategy, joining the Youth League of the African National Congress (ANC). The government retaliated with a treason trial against its main opponents, Mandela among them, which dragged on for five years. By that time the country had been convulsed by the massacre of peaceful black demonstrators at Sharpeville in March 1960. Most liberation movements, including the ANC, were banned. Mandela shifted to a stance of armed resistance as the ANC went underground, and he traveled extensively abroad to enlist support.

Soon after his return, he was arrested and sentenced to imprisonment on Robben Island. Mandela was hauled from prison to face, with other arrested ANC leaders, an almost certain death sentence. His statement from the dock electrified South Africa and resonated around the world: "During my lifetime I have dedicated myself to the struggle of the African people. I have fought against white domination, and I have fought against black domination. I have cherished the ideal of a democratic and free society in which all persons live together in harmony and with equal opportunities. It is an ideal which I hope to live for and to achieve. But, if needs be, it is an ideal for which I am prepared to die."

After more than two decades in prison, the most famous prisoner in the world was escorted, in the greatest secrecy, to the state president's office to start negotiating not only his own release but also the nation's transition from apartheid to democracy.

To the surprise of many, Mandela shifted his former hard-line position to one of reconciliation. At one dramatic meeting of the two sides, he had musical groups play the other sides' anthems. Subsequently it was a struggle for Mandela to both keep his own supporters and to allay white fears. But his patience, wisdom, and the visionary quality Mandela brought to his struggle—above all the moral integrity with which he set about to unify a divided people—resulted in the country's first democratic elections and his selection as President.

Muhammad Ali later wrote: "Mandela is my hero because he embraces all people like brothers and sisters. He is one of the greatest civil rights leaders in world history. Mandela is my hero because his spirit cannot be crushed."

A lot of people are
waiting for Martin Luther King
or Mahatma Gandhi to come back
—but they are gone. We are it.
It is up to us. It is up to you.
MARIAN WRIGHT EDELMAN

CHAPTER TEN

Taste the Power of Commitment

The great stand apart from the ordinary by the depth of their commitment fueled by their faith in the human spirit.

W HAT MOST OF US SPEND OUR LIVES THINKING ABOUT IS what I call outcomes. How do I get more love? How do I get more recognition? How do I get more comfort in my life? How do I get more money? How do I get more of the things that are important to me? Isn't it interesting that some people have so much more of what we want than we do? They have created more of these outcomes. Why do these people have more? It's a really simple answer. Some people are more committed to those things than others. The reason why they have more is that they are more committed to getting it.

I seek out and enjoy immensely performances that show commitment to excellence in many arenas of life from art to sports. I think of Karen Briggs and Shardad Rohani playing a violin duet with Yanni and London's Royal Philharmonic Orchestra in the 2000-year-old Herod Atticus Theatre in Athens, Greece, that became the live concert album "Yanni Live at the Acropolis." When the amazing duet was over, I noticed tears streaming down most of the faces in the audience because of the rare excellence of the performance.

I love events of any kind and have attended a zillion sports events. I notice the commitment of athletes both at college and professional levels because talent is wonderful, my friends, but you can't choose to have talent. You can choose to have commitment.

For me commitment was Magic Johnson. In the 80s I had season tickets at the Forum. I got to watch all those battles every year and every year it was L.A. versus Boston. When Magic Johnson would come out, I could see there was something special about him. If the Lakers needed 35 points, he would score 35 points. If they needed assists, he would get 20 assists. If they needed rebounds, he would go in, even though he was a guard and get the rebounds. He was amazing. When he walked on the court, every one of the other players, not only on his team but also on the other team, played differently. You may say, maybe the superstars are just born with something the rest of us don't have. But watch. Michael Jordan. Every night at the end of practice while everyone else went and showered and complained about how hard they were working, he would stand and shoot 1,000 free throws every night before he left the court. He took the last 100 shots with a blindfold on or with his eyes closed. Do you know how long it takes to shoot 1,000 free throws? That's commitment.

Tiger Woods. There's something special about him, too. He has changed the game of golf. He has changed the look of golfers. They all used to be big bellies, a bunch of fat white guys walking down the course hitting the ball around. I saw Tiger when he was in college at Stanford University. In fact, he was on the float at the Rose Bowl in 1995, the chiropractic centennial year. Tiger was the celebrity as the Stanford golfer on the front of the chiropractic float going along Pasadena Avenue. He was a skinny guy. You see him walking down the course now. He has that beam of an athlete. Broad shoulders, thin waist. They say that every morning he gets up at four o'clock and lifts weights for a couple of hours. A golfer lifting weights! You notice that now everyone else is getting buffed up just to be able to stay in the game with him. Then he goes out and hits five hundred balls with one club.

This has personal meaning to me. I decided to take up golf years ago. I went to the driving range, and they asked, do you want the small, medium, or large bucket. I said I'd take the barrel. So they gave me this barrel that had maybe a hundred balls in it. I went out there and whacked the ball a hundred times and tore up all the intercostal muscles and couldn't lift a golf club again for a year. Tiger hits five hundred balls with one club. Then he goes on the putting green, and he putts a hundred putts in a row. If he misses one, he starts over again. Wow. What if we were that committed in our lives with our kids and our businesses? That kind of commitment shows up as excellence in whatever part of life we decide to be extraordinary.

Commitment Trumps Talent

Besides sports, I love movies. And so it's no surprise that I love sports movies. And it just happens that one of the great examples of team commitment is in the movie *Miracle*. It's the story of the 1980 U.S. Olympic ice hockey team's improbable performance. It's an absolutely true story where the screenwriters used the moment of commitment as the turning point in the dramatic structure of the film. That moment of commitment set up the team's ability to prevail. Coach Herb Brooks had to pit an assortment of young college players who had not gone pro against the veteran Soviet team of essentially professional players who had *never* lost the gold medal. Brooks didn't have players with the greatest talent in the country; he certainly didn't have an experienced team, and he didn't have much time. He committed himself, single-mindedly—and to the detriment of his marriage—to this Olympic effort. He decided to build his champion team by instilling—guess what? Commitment. Did he talk to them about commitment? No. Instead he used an intriguing strategy.

Individual commitment to a group effort—that is what makes a team work, a company work, a society work, a civilization work.

VINCE LOMBARDI

Early on, Coach Brooks asked several players in a casual way, "Who do you play for?" One would say U. Mass. And one would say Minnesota. A few days later he'd ask some other guys, and they'd name their college teams. This went on intermittently for weeks.

At one evening practice, he put the players through rigorous skating drills for hours on end. In one drill, the team skated at top speed down the ice and at a whistle signal, they had to reverse direction with hip-wrenching abruptness, and skate back at top speed. Again. Again. Again, until as viewers we were exhausted and the players were near collapse. At Brooks' signal, the assistant coach would blow the whistle and the drill was repeated. The endless sprint-and-turn, sprint-and-turn, was so painful to watch that the assistant coach could hardly bring himself to blow the whistle and finally had to turn over the whistle and go outside. Brooks kept the guys going. Every now and then he would stop and ask a player, "Who do you play for?" The guy would say, "Dartmouth" or whatever, and the whistle would blow again and they were careening down the ice again, digging in at every turn, spraying ice. Finally, when Brooks paused and asked a player "Who do you play for?" the guy said, "The United States Olympic Team." Brooks said, "Thank you, gentlemen." And he let them go to bed without another word spoken. At that moment they became a team. The guys committed not to anything in their former lives, not to the loyalties and habits and aspirations and level of performance of their former lives, but to this team, this moment, this level, this Olympic vision of victory.

As the story played out, the players' commitment to each other was their strength against their highly trained, battled-hardened Soviet opponents. After one frantic final barrage of Soviet shots, stopped by goalie Jim Craig, the buzzer sounded and the U.S. had beaten the Soviets 4 to 3. The victory not only sent the team on to win the Gold Medal round against Finland but, according to one reporter, brought the whole country "out of a decade of gloom and despair."

Commit to the team—your community, your family, your profession—and along with the team you can realize your vision.

Who can forget Kerri Strug, who in the 1996 Atlanta Olympics was part of the team competition in gymnastics? The U.S. had a lead over Russia and was on its way to picking up its first gold in the team combined exercises. Then teammate Dominique Moceanu fell on both her vaults and Strug fell on her first vault. A hush fell over the 32,000 spectators, mostly Americans. Strug had felt a pop in her ankle when she fell and she could barely walk back to her seat. If she didn't make the next vault and stick the landing, it would be good-bye gold. But how could she sprint down the runway, propel her body into the air over the horse, and land upright on one good leg?

"Kerri, listen to me. You can do it," said USA coach Bela Karolyi. Strug had to forget the leg, forget the surgery that would follow, forget the pain. Just go with the commitment to the team.

Strug gritted her teeth, ran at top speed down the runway,

launched her body into the air, and stuck the landing before collapsing on the floor in pain.

Who can forget the image of the grinning Coach Karolyi, who gathered Strug in his arms and carried her to the award ceremony where the crowd stood in noisy appreciation for her guts and commitment? The two torn ligaments in her ankle prevented her from competing in any individual events in that Olympic Games.

Commit to the Team, and the Team Commits to You

I remember another instance of injury and team commitment closer to my home then. In the 1990s, Mike McLaughlin, a center on the Stanford University football team, set a goal for himself to become the first Stanford offensive lineman to start every game of his career since that feat had been accomplished a decade before. It wasn't a world record; it was just that young man's vision for those four years.

McLaughlin started regularly and performed admirably, but in his 30th game he suffered a bad sprain in a game against Oregon State. Doctor's orders were to stay off his injured foot for several weeks. He did not practice prior to the next game 12 days later, but when the first ball was snapped, he was there. He wanted that record and the team, the coach, and the fans wanted it for him. So they taped his ankle till it was immobile and he hobbled out on the field. The fans roared when his name was called. He played sparingly with a sophomore taking most of the snaps, but he played.

The 305-pound center from San Jose went on to attain his record of starting all 44 games of his career thanks to his commitment and the cooperation of his team. Along the way he was named First-Team All-Pacific-10 Conference in 1999 by TSN and was front and center in the 1999-2000 Rose Bowl, Stanford's first trip to the Rose Bowl in 28 years. That was the outcome of commitment to excellence and to the team.

As much as I love sports and the drama commitment brings to competition, I'll have to admit that being paid big bucks, signing bonuses, endorsement money, or athletic scholarships would seem to make commitment easier; and if there's no money, there's the roar of the crowd, the magazine covers, the trophies, the TV interviews, and the Wheaties box. You might say, "For what Tiger Woods is paid, I'd be committed, too."

The purest commitment comes when no one is paying you and when you're making a sacrifice in order to make your vision become a reality.

Commitment Requires Sacrifice

Famous political leaders like Nelson Mandela, Mohandas Gandhi, Vaclav Havel and Lech Walesa all had a grand vision, put their vision into words, changed the paradigm of their nation or people, committed their lives to a cause, sacrificed their own freedom, and risked their lives to make their vision a reality.

Nelson Mandela was imprisoned for 28 years for his activities against apartheid in his native South Africa and for equal opportunity. He said, "I have cherished the ideal of a democratic and free society in which all persons live together in harmony and with equal opportunities. It is an ideal which I hope to live to achieve. But if need be, it is an ideal for which I am prepared to die." Sentenced to life imprisonment for his activities, he was offered freedom more than once in exchange for accepting that his home region be set aside for blacks only and that he live there quietly, in other words, publicly accept apartheid. Mandela refused. When asked to denounce violence on behalf of his cause in exchange for freedom, he said, "Prisoners cannot enter into contracts. Only free men can negotiate." He refused the offer. After 28 years of imprisonment, he was released. Soon afterwards, he did denounce violence as a free man. He went on to lead his country out of apartheid and was awarded the 1993 Nobel Peace Prize for his role.

Similarly, Mohandas Gandhi, through his philosophy of nonviolence and his passion for independence for India, began a drive for freedom that doomed colonialism. During World War II, through his Quit India movement, he resisted the rule of Great Britain by leading mass civil disobedience and nonviolent resistance. Imprisoned from 1942 to 1944, he became so ill with malaria that he was released because the government feared he would die in prison and become a martyr for Indian independence. Free, he became "Father of the Nation" as Britain, seeing the writing on the wall, started the process of independence for India. After independence, Gandhi worked against caste discrimination, for women's rights, and for peace between India's religious groups.

Vaclav Havel, as a playwright in communist-controlled Czechoslovakia, sacrificed much for his vision of civil rights and freedom. Following the suppression of the Prague Spring in 1968, a period of relative freedom of the press and artistic expression, Havel was banned from the theatre. Becoming more politically active and passionate about nonviolent resistance, he was imprisoned several times, once for more than four years. His part in the Velvet Revolution of 1989 led to free elections and his presidency of the nation until the breakup of Czechoslovakia.

Lech Walesa, a leader of shipyard workers in Poland as the Soviet

Union's control waned, risked his life and was often "detained" as he began to organize independent trade unions. He called strikes to protest unfair policies that crippled the Polish economy and he formed a federation of unions called Solidarity. His vision gradually was realized in Poland when censorship was lightened and reforms allowed freedom of association. Solidarity eventually became a political party and was legalized. In 1983, Walesa received the Nobel Peace Prize. The Nobel Committee said:

The solidarity for which he is spokesman is an expression of precisely the concept of being at one with humanity; therefore he belongs to us all. The world has heard his voice and understood his message; the Nobel Peace Prize is merely a confirmation of this.

Lech Walesa has made the name 'Solidarity' more than an expression of the unity of a group campaigning for special interests. Solidarity has come to represent the determination to resolve conflicts and obliterate disagreement through peaceful negotiation, where all involved meet with a mutual respect for one another's integrity.

I quote this portion of the Committee's remarks as a reminder of how a great vision requires the power of words as well as acts of commitment to be realized. Indeed, the word "solidarity" came to have great power.

Dr. Martin Luther King, Jr., was another activist who translated his vision of equal rights for black people into words and was committed to putting them before his people over and over, very aware that he might be killed for his work and his words. In his last speech in Memphis, he expressed his expectation of losing his life before his cause succeeded; his words presaged imminent death. Yet death was not more powerful than King's commitment to civil rights.

We All Have the Potential

So maybe you can't see the relevance of these stories to your life. Maybe you can't picture yourself being a Gandhi or a Mandela. I'm here to tell you we all have the potential for commitment to our vision, no matter what our circumstances.

I saw a story in the *Los Angeles Times* when I was living there. On the front page of the metro section of the Sunday paper was a full-page story with pictures about a woman who gives $2,500 a year to her church. I'm thinking, "That's nice, but does it warrant a full-page spread on the front of the metro section running over to the back page?" It was right around the time when Ted Turner gave a billion dollars to UNICEF and Bill Gates had given a billion dollars to his favorite causes. I'd thought, "Man, those guys have commitment." I read on. The woman only makes $23,000 a year. I have to tell you, I have lived in L.A., and I know what it costs to live there. I lived in a 1,600-square-foot house with another 1,600 square feet of space outside and it cost a half a million dollars in 1984. I am reading this and I am thinking, "$23,000?" You can't even buy car insurance when you're making just $23,000." In fact, the next paragraph said this woman cannot have a car. She cannot have a house. She has to live in an apartment close to her church and her work so that she can walk there because, if she didn't do that, she would not have the $2,500 dollars a year to donate to her church. Then it dawned on me: Which is the bigger commitment, a billion dollars to UNICEF when you have multiple billions or $2,500 a year when you are only making $23,000? Everyone has the potential for commitment.

I told you earlier about Metropolitan Serenity House (MASH), the residential treatment center for young men addicted to drugs and alcohol. I told you it was one of the few places that the guys who relapse are not kicked out. There are a lot of reasons: Relapse is part of the disease and part of learning what it takes to recover, and these guys are young. But how many times can you keep taking a guy back who keeps going out and getting high and stealing to get money to pay for the drugs? The answer, founder Anne Bush Ambrose says, is "as many times as it takes."

MASH takes them back as many times as they ask for help and commit themselves to recovery. There's that word commitment. The commitment involves everyone in the system. First, when the young man and his family come to seek admission to Serenity House, the staff tries to assess the young man's commitment to recovery. Does he really want to give up drugs at this time? Sometimes the staff says, "If you don't want to give up drugs, don't. Go out and use them until you're done with it. Then come back to us for help." They make the kid work a little bit to get accepted for treatment. They are looking for commitment from him, but they realize the kid is in trouble and will therefore say one thing and change his mind easily and he doesn't really know his mind. Getting to know himself is part of the treatment. But if he'll even make an effort to try to convince the staff that he's committed to sobriety, he may be a good candidate.

They look more closely at the parents. Will they commit to long-term treatment, will they commit to regular family therapy, coming every other weekend even from a long distance? The young men whose families commit to learning and changing through therapy and education are the ones who succeed in recovering and going on to contribute to society. If the young addict and his family commit to the extent that they are able and they become a part of the Serenity House community, MASH commits to them.

This commitment has meant that, when Ambrose hears from a MASH guy in relapse—she's the first person they call when they are in trouble—she goes to the worst parts of town and picks them up, accompanies them to the hospital for detox or to be treated when their drug dealer beats them up for not having money to pay. She gives them comfort in jail, or wherever they land. She talks on their behalf to the police, judges and parole officers. (Her work in providing treatment instead of incarceration for addicts has won her the Liberty Bell Award from the Georgia Bar Association.) She takes them to her house and lets them sleep on her sofa until she can work things out so that they can be readmitted to the MASH community. She does this as often and for as long as it takes. Many of these young men have, largely because of her commitment, become outstanding citizens in recovery, college graduates, prized employees and mentors to other addicts. "Don't quit before the miracle happens" is one of her mottos.

Faith in the Human Spirit

What sustains commitment is faith in the human spirit to prevail, to heal and to soar. Read on. There's a wonderful couple in upstate New York named Barry and Samahria (also called Suzi) Kaufman. They had two beautiful daughters born to them, then finally the son they'd waited for to complete the family. They named him Raun. A short period of time after his birth, they realized that something was wrong with this child. He became very unresponsive. He ignored people, and didn't like to be held. Most of his waking time was spent sitting in a room staring at a spot on the ceiling and rocking back and forth endlessly. Of course, they had this child evaluated. The best experts in the world confirmed the Kaufmans' own diagnosis of severe autism. Some said that early intervention was important, but they didn't work with children as young as Raun. Others said it didn't matter when they began treatment because such children sink deeper and deeper into isolation without socialization or language, regardless of treatment.

The Kaufmans realized they were on their own. They observed that Raun, at 17 months, seemed perfectly happy in his trance-like isolation; they speculated that this happiness was key; that a lot of the angry behavior of autistic children who were institutionalized stemmed from people forcing the children out of the state of happiness in which they enveloped themselves. They would not do that to Raun.

Aerodynamically the bumblebee shouldn't be able to fly, but the bumblebee doesn't know that so it goes on flying anyway.

MARY KAY ASH

They would respect the behavior that gave him that peace. They also adopted a particular spiritual underpinning to sustain their deep love for their child whether or not his condition improved. They let go of the outcome. They would show their love for Raun by loving who he was at each moment regardless of what the future might hold.

How could they get that love and acceptance across to a child who at this point had no communication whatsoever with the external world? What they decided to do was mimic Raun's behavior all day long, hoping that by mimicking maybe something would get through to that perfect little boy on the inside to let him know that they thought he was okay. So they actually stripped a bathroom in their house and got rid of all the external environmental stresses that he might encounter. In this simplified environment, as Barry recalls poignantly in his 1976 book *Son-Rise*, they painstakingly introduced "a program of instruction for him by breaking down each activity, each event, into small and digestible parts," each of which might build a new pathway in his brain. Then Samahria quit her other activities and sat alone in that bathroom with Raun eight or nine hours a day. If he just stared at the light on the ceiling, she sat and stared at the light on the ceiling with him. If he rocked, then she rocked in rhythm with him back and forth on the floor of that bathroom. Whatever he did, she showed him it was worthy of her imitation.

They found only one complex activity that seemed to interest Raun. Even before he was a year and a half, he would deftly spin a plate on the floor like you spin a nickel on a tabletop. Raun would stand up over the plate, watching it, rocking slightly in unison with it, losing himself in the motion as if in meditation, "a great and skilled activity performed by a very little boy for a very great and expectant audience—himself." So they allowed him this self-soothing, even encouraged it. They brought him an array of plates and pans to spin. He would spin and stare. They would spin and stare. They enlisted their daughters and friends of the family to spin and sit and stare. Still Samahria spent eight hours a day alone with him, imitating his actions and his inaction and gradually moving closer and closer to him until he allowed her to touch him without recoiling.

Over the weeks, she learned every glance of possible interest he exhibited, every nuance of his motion. She began to touch and stroke him. He never acknowledged her existence with a response, communication, or even eye contact. But he did learn to tolerate her touch, and through her touch she tried to humanize his interaction with inanimate objects, which he preferred to humans.

She never went beyond what he clearly tolerated. Gradually, in sessions that filled 75 hours a week, Samahria taught him to follow a cookie with his eyes; she played with him in water, mud and grass, labeling each object and each act with words. She introduced additional stimuli like music. Although he'd often appeared deaf and took no notice of sound, Raun seemed to enjoy music. Samahria would turn a record player on, and Raun would respond by swaying to the rhythm.

How long do you think you could keep that up? How many weeks do you think you might be able to spend eight hours in a bathroom with a child who didn't acknowledge your existence?

One day in the bathroom Raun apparently wanted the music on; he stood by the silent player and stared at it. Then he went and stood in front of Samahria and for the first time looked directly into her eyes. There was no sound or gesture, but Samahria, who knew every glint of his eyes by heart, realized that he had at last connected her with the beginning of the music. By standing in front of her, motionless and silent, he was expressing a want and he was acknowledging her existence and connection to what he wanted. A magnificent breakthrough! She jumped up and turned on the music. He at last had discovered a means of controlling his universe and it involved interaction, however minuscule, with another person. This vital piece of the puzzle was followed, not by a flood of progress, but by painstakingly tiny steps using that single piece of the puzzle. The Kaufmans could now use Raun's wants to shape his learning. In his 14th week of their intensive program, Raun spoke his first meaningful syllable to ask for water.

Language as communication!

By age two-and-a-half, Raun, "loving, happy and creative," could speak in sentences of up to 14 words and could spell up to 50 words. His family continued to work with him for 75 hours a week. I tell you this story to make clear to you the nature and rewards of commitment.

That kid went on to graduate from high school and attend college. Thirty years later Barry wrote a sequel to the story called *Son-Rise: The Miracle Continues* with a view of the miracle written by Raun himself. The vision that Samahria and Barry had for their little boy, the vision that they made into a reality through the power of commitment, has helped other autistic children through work the Kaufmans have done with the family's educational foundation, The Option Institute and Fellowship, based in Sheffield, Mass.

100 Percent or Zero: Your Choice

Commitment is what produces these outcomes in our lives. You say, "Well how come some people are so much more committed to things than others?" It's real simple. I have looked at this for 30 years, and I can only come up with one thing. You get to choose. The Kaufmans got to choose whether to commit 75 hours a week for weeks and months and years or to institutionalize their son. It's a choice. You get to choose where to expend your time, energy and money. Where are you going to be committed?

I love it when students come up to me sometimes and say, "Dr. Riekeman, I am going to make you proud with straight A's this quarter." At the end of the quarter some of them don't make it. I say, "What happened?" If you look at their lives, you see they have spent eight hours a night watching TV. Were they committed to making straight A's? No, they were not. They were committed to watching eight hours of TV in the evening. All you have to do is look where people put their time, effort, energy, money and other resources. That is what they are really committed to.

You get to choose on a moment-to-moment basis how you will show up in Grand Central Station. You get to choose how great your commitment is going to be and what it is going to be for. Based upon that commitment, you will get certain outcomes. You will have an extraordinary life or you won't.

Let me tell you another story about commitment because there's a quote involved that I like a lot. At the outbreak of World War II, a Scotsman named William H. Murray, a mountain climber by avocation, joined the Argyll and Sutherland Highlanders and was posted to the Middle East and North Africa, where he was captured in the desert. He then spent three years as a Prisoner of War in Italy, Germany, and Czechoslovakia. While imprisoned, he wrote a book entitled *Mountaineering in Scotland*. He was putting his vision of mountaineering into words to encourage people and inspire them to preserve the pristine mountains of Scotland. It wasn't easy writing this book. The first draft of the work was written on the only paper available to him—rough toilet paper. Near its completion, the manuscript was found and destroyed by the Gestapo. To the amazement of his fellow prisoners, Murray's response to the loss was to start again, despite the continuing risk of the book's being seized and in spite of the fact that his physical condition was so poor from the near starvation diet that he believed he would never climb a mountain again. The man understood commitment. He could choose to commit himself to the book or he could choose to abandon the project in the face of obstacles. The completed work was finally pub-

> *Commitment can be best illustrated by a breakfast of ham and eggs. The chicken was involved, the pig was committed.*
>
> ANONYMOUS

173

lished in 1947.

After the war, Murray did recover, and he became strong enough to climb mountains. In fact, he tackled the big one: Mount Everest. Murray later wrote what he thought about commitment in the following account of the 1951 Everest Reconnaissance Expedition, for which he was Deputy Leader:

> *We had definitely committed ourselves and were halfway out of our ruts. We had put down our passage money—booked a sailing to Bombay. This may sound too simple, but is great in consequence. Until one is committed, there is hesitancy, the chance to draw back, always ineffectiveness. Concerning all acts of initiative (and creation), there is one elementary truth the ignorance of which kills countless ideas and splendid plans: that the moment one definitely commits oneself, then providence moves too. A whole stream of events issues from the decision, raising in one's favor all manner of unforeseen incidents, meetings and material assistance, which no man could have dreamt would have come his way." [William H. Murray,* The Scottish Himalaya Expedition, *1951]*

And then he adds these famous lines attributed to Goethe: "Whatever you can or dream you can, begin it. Boldness has genius, power and magic in it."

Commitment. Begin now. When you show up in Grand Central Station, put down your passage money for an extraordinary life.

COMMITMENT BRINGS SUCCESS

- It's easy to see that sports heroes and others who accomplish great things have talent. The fact is, though, that their talent is always fulfilled by commitment—sacrifice, practice and hard work.

- Why do some people commit themselves and others, perhaps with more talent and resources, fail to do so? It comes down to making a choice.

- Often beginning a course of commitment seems to generate resources for success that never could have been imagined. Keep climbing and Providence gives you a helping hand.

MAKE YOUR LIFE EXT...

CHAPTER   TITLE

**11   FIRST BE COACHABLE,
THEN BE A COACH**

:: POWERFUL PEOPLE ARE COACHABLE

:: YOU TOO CAN HAVE A COACH

:: DISNEY VALUES

*It is a paradoxical but
profoundly true and important
principle of life that the most likely
way to reach a goal is to be aiming
not at that goal itself but at some
more ambitious goal beyond it.*

ARNOLD TOYNBEE

CHAPTER ELEVEN

First Be Coachable,
Then Be a Coach

Try selecting your personal board of trustees. When you face
a decision, think about what they would tell you.

POWERFUL PEOPLE, PEOPLE WHO TURN THEIR VISION INTO reality, are coachable, and powerful people coach others so that their vision grows.

Remember the sports stars I offered in the last chapter as examples of commitment? They had a vision of excellence and victory, and they were committed to that vision. What else did they have? Great coaches! And the athletes were coachable. Yes, they had talent and desire of their own, but a coach was there to hold them accountable, to guide, to acknowledge their successes and to point out their errors. As long-time Dallas Cowboys coach Tom Landry once said about coaching, "Leadership is getting someone to do what they don't want to do, to achieve what they want to achieve." So Landry, during his NFL-record 20 consecutive winning seasons, demanded of his players that they do what they might not have done without him to get the outcomes they all wanted. Instructing teaches the strategies and moves of the game; coaching pushes talented athletes to extraordinary performances by insisting they do what they already know how to do.

Powerful People Are Coachable

What about the rest of us who don't have Tom Landry or Vince Lombardi or Vince Dooley at our side? Powerful people seek out coaches—parents, heroes and mentors, as well as professional coaches. Powerful people use models of life lessons so they don't have to learn everything the hard way. They listen to wise people. They ask wise people to listen to them as they put their vision into words, so that they can clarify their vision before they put these words out into the world where they will influence others. Powerful people don't go it alone.

The political figures I've talked about in previous chapters, who have risen from obscurity to lead world-changing movements—have also had their models and mentors and coaches. Sometimes these coaches were there in person, sometimes in spirit. *Time* magazine, naming Gandhi as runner up for Person of the 20th Century, named the following activists for human rights: Dalai Lama; Lech Walesa; Dr. Martin Luther King, Jr.; Cesar Chavez; Aung San Suu Kyi; Benigno Aquino, Jr.; Desmond Tutu; and Nelson Mandela as "Children of Gandhi" and his spiritual heirs to the tradition of non-violence. People today who may know nothing about Gandhi know about his spiritual successors, and so the legacy of non-violent resistance to injustice goes on.

You Too Can Have a Coach

Like sports stars and the social and political activists, you can have a coach to help you discover or refine your vision and move more efficiently towards making your vision a reality. Here at Life University we believe in coaching as a part of our mission strongly enough that we are beginning a course in life and career coaching for each of our students of chiropractic so that when they graduate they will also be certified as life coaches by the International Coach Federation.

You can benefit from hiring a coach if you are ready to move forward toward an extraordinary life and if you are coachable. My colleague Dr. Janice Hughes of The Masters Circle says, "Being coachable is a skill. I know since I'm a professional coach. Powerful people realize that, not matter what they have attained or achieved, by being coachable they tap into more of the power within themselves. They are willing to try things. They don't say, 'That's a good idea but....' Coachable people realize the power of outside input and knowledge, and then utilize it."

Even if you don't have your own professional coach, you can think of whom you admire most and actively develop a mentoring relationship, formal or informal, with them. You can read or listen to the words of your role models because, as powerful people they have used the power of words. Most leaders have written books or made videos, and books have been written and films made about them. Make a list: Some of your favorites who have changed your life in some measure are _____.

Every year additional powerful people functioning as coaches publish new books. A book that changed my life may not change yours because you aren't ready for it or you've passed it or because a particular approach or style doesn't speak to you. But another time, another book will spin you around and shake your life into a new paradigm.

I think of a 2005 tragedy in Atlanta, which was brought to closure in large part by a book. Brian Nichols, a man brought into the Fulton County Courthouse for trial for rape, broke loose from guards, seized a weapon, and killed several people including senior Judge Rowland

Barnes, a court recorder and a sheriff's deputy. Nichols fled from the courthouse, killing another person in the street. He ended up holding hostage Ashley Smith, a young woman herself troubled by drug use. Among many things that went on between them as Smith tried to survive this captivity in her own apartment, she read to Nichols from the book *The Purpose-Driven Life*, a book she was reading to help herself find a better way. He was impressed by her empathy and apparently by the book.

"I wanted to see my little girl the next morning and I didn't want him to hurt anybody else," Ashley told CBS News *Early Show* co-anchor Harry Smith. "And I knew that if I talked to him in the right way that he wouldn't." The power of words. Ashley Smith listened, accepted what she heard, reflected it back, and moved the killer forward in his thinking. Ashley Smith seems to have been a born coach with the right book in her hands at the right time.

My chief want in life is someone who shall make me do what I can.

RALPH WALDO EMERSON

Many books have changed lives, though rarely have the changes been distilled into one such dramatic scene. Letitia says that a long time ago *Children the Challenge* by Rudolf Dreikurs and Vicki Soltz changed her in ways that went beyond parenting. Recently one of her coaching clients suddenly escaped from the grasp of personal fear having read only 57 pages of Neale Donald Walsch's *Conversations with God*.

In the same way, I hope that for some of you the words in this book will strike a chord and set you off towards an extraordinary life. In fact, I have received letters from people who have heard my words and have changed their vision and their careers because of them. The power of words is great for those who are coachable.

And you can also have your own internalized team of coaches, a sort of virtual board of trustees whom you ask the most important questions and who, like a professional coach, will help you find the answers that lie within you.

A business or a nonprofit organization seeks for its board people of stature who bring different strengths and skills to the table: Someone who knows about money, someone who knows about legal matters and liability, someone who knows about marketing or the business of the organization such as art or education, or social services. A board also needs people who have money and know people with money, who have influence and know people with influence. Similarly, on your own virtual board of trustees you will have someone with these strengths or with the particular strengths you need.

On my personal board of trustees, I have my grandson, the one who announced that his penis floats. He's the one on my board who looks at things in a different way, who notices the obvious that everyone else is missing. I ask him, "What's another way to look at this situation." And he blurts out the answer I should have seen for myself. I'd turn to him if I was stuck and wanted to find a new way of looking at things or if I wanted to be playful because being serious all the time makes a dull boy. I'd turn to him if I wanted to interact with a child or understand a child.

Just as a board member doesn't have to be an adult, it doesn't have to be human either. In fact on my board I have a chicken that I saw on a *20/20* special with Hugh Downs and Barbara Walters. The show was about brutality to animals in the food industry. It showed a chicken farm in Hungary with cages stacked from the floor right to the ceiling with little aisles where workers could walk up and down. Running up and down these aisles were conveyer belts. The chickens were in cages that were so small they couldn't stand up, could not even turn around in the cage. All their food was carried to them on the conveyer belts. Their waste products and the eggs were carried away on the conveyer belts, which accumulated down at the end. The room was temperature- and light-controlled: Because chickens lay eggs at sun up, they would shorten the time periods in between simulated dawn hours to get more eggs out of the chicken. Obviously raising animals like this produces stress, and these chickens became so neurotic in these cages, they pecked themselves to death. So they had to be constantly replacing them from the hatchery.

In the little hatchery there were six workers in white uniforms. Three on each side of a four-foot-wide conveyer belt next to some incubators and, as the eggs hatched, they would dump dozens of chicks out of the incubators onto this conveyer belt. As they moved down the belt, the workers would sort them. They would get rid of the unhealthy ones. They were also sorting these chickens by sex because they didn't want males in those cages that they can't get eggs from. They put the unhealthy chicks and the males in a trash bin that they would come and clean out every now and then and take off to a compactor.

If you grew up on a farm as I did, you know that every now and then there was a little black chicken born. There was this little black chick on this conveyer belt, and it stood out in this mass of yellow like a sore thumb. This little black chicken didn't know that he was headed for the dumpster and the compactor. All he knew was he wanted to be with the other chicks at the other end of the conveyer belt. So he oriented himself and ran down the belt. The first worker, without even breaking her rhythm, saw him coming out of the corner of her eye and she smacked him. He rolled end over end and stopped just before he fell into the trashcan. He picked himself up, oriented himself, and then headed back down the conveyer belt. Three times he did this. The last time she really smacked him hard because she was irritated. He rolled end over end and fell into the trashcan. Someone came along and picked up the bin. This worker took it and put a bunch of other trash in the bin and put it into a big compactor, which compacted it into a big square piece of matter. They put it on a truck with other big pieces of square matter and hauled it off to the woods and dumped it.

The credits were starting to roll at the end of this show. I am a pretty philosophical guy, and I was trying to decide why were they showing me this. So I was waiting for them to cut back to Hugh Downs in New York to see what point he was going to make. Then all of a sudden this last credit ran by, and I saw one of these piles of trash jiggle just a little bit and the camera zoomed in. This little black head stuck itself out from this mass of dead matter, pulled its damp body out, looked around, jumped on a little country road, and scurried off into the woods.

You know what that little black chick taught me? You don't have to have the solutions to all the problems in the world. You don't have to know how to dig out of every problem for yourself, your children or humanity. All you have to do is get up every day and do the best you can on the conveyer belt. Get up and do the very best you can with commitment, vision and integrity on the conveyer belt.

That little black chick is always there on my board of trustees when the going gets rough. I say, "Little Black Chick, tell me what you were thinking that day? And the chick says, I was thinking, "Get your head up. Put your foot out, then your other foot. Then run like hell." And I say, "Thank you, Little Black Chick. That's what I'll do today."

Disney Values

Another member of my board is my mentor Walt Disney. When he was first getting started, long before he built the Disney empire, he took his daughter to Griffith Park in Los Angeles. Griffith Park has more than 4,400 acres right in the middle of Los Angeles. You can hike and camp there. There's a zoo and the Hollywood Bowl, and there's a beautiful carousel there, unless they tore it down. Walt and his daughter went to the zoo, ate hot dogs and stuff, and finished the day by riding the carousel. Walt remembered three things about the day. First, he bought cotton candy and the cotton candy was limp. The second thing he remembered was the bench he was sitting on had been chipped and painted so many times that not only was it uncomfortable but, when he stood up, he actually snagged his pants. The third thing is his daughter went to ride the carousel and she happened to get on the one horse that was broken that day, and it wasn't going up and down. Walt Disney sat there and swore right then that some day he was going to create a family entertainment empire where the cotton candy was always fresh, the benches were always clean and comfortable, and all the horses always went up and down.

Years later, a hamburger chain, I've been told, was trying to model its business management procedures after Disney's empire. So this hamburger chain decided to steal Disney's office policy manual. They got the document and opened it up. Here's what the office policy manual said: "The cotton candy is always fresh, the benches are always clean and comfortable to sit on, and all the horses will always go up and down."

The hamburger flippers couldn't figure it out. They thought, gosh, he needs to have information about solvents to clean windows, and what kind of middle management people you need to check up on, lower management to check on the workers and how many workers you need, and when should they clean up the windows, and how frequently should the bathrooms be repainted. Can you imagine how thick the manual would be if you had to have every situation defined to run the busy empire? Disney had one page: The cotton candy is always fresh, the benches are always clean and comfortable to sit on, and all the horses will always go up and down. And when I wonder what to do in my own life, I think about this manual and I put this kind of excellence into whatever project concerns me.

Walt Disney also said something like this: Whenever you get ready to run your business, the first thing you should do is to sit down with the people you're going to work with and define your value system. What do you believe in, what does your business stand for? Your value system will determine all your decisions, he said, and once you have your values defined, the second thing you do is set up some very simple absolute standards. His standards, of course, were that cotton candy was always fresh, the benches were always clean and comfortable to sit on, and all the horses always go up and down. Do those two things—define your values and set standards—and you'll wind up with an end product that most people call goals.

> *It's not hard to make decisions when you know what your values are.*
> ROY DISNEY

For decades, the major theme in the business community has been management by goals. Some people called it management by objectives or by statistics. You ask yourself what are our goals this year: We want to have this many new patients each month, we want to make this much money, and we want to increase our profit. You sit down and lay out your goals for your family, and you lay out goals for your spiritual congregation. You lay out some goals about where you want to be in six months or a year in any area of life. Then you set up some statistics to monitor whether or not you're reaching your goals, and then you manage your business by the goals and statistics of your objectives. Some of us in the business community threw that method out decades ago.

We adopted the philosophy that Walt Disney always had. It's called management by values. Let me tell you why Walt Disney was never obsessed with management by goals. He says that whenever people set goals and go about the process of reaching them, he says when they get there, the goals usually weren't what they thought they were going to be when they started off. See, this is, gosh, just three more years and I'll have my driver's license. Gosh, just two more years and I'll be out of high school. Gosh, just four more years, and I can go out and get a real job and a real car. And then when we get there, we say, "Oh, we made it, but is that all there is?" And so eventually we quit setting these goals and become cynical.

Walt Disney never put goals first. Does that mean Walt Disney never set goals? No, Walt Disney set goals. His goals fit into the bigger picture called management by values. When people set out to reach goals without being clear on what their value system is, then in the process of obtaining these goals, more than likely they compromise their values without even knowing it. They give up some of their selves to get them.

What were Walt Disney's values? Family entertainment. Did you know that Walt Disney never made an R-rated film? Even though traditionally R-rated films gross three times as much money as G-rated films do. Walt Disney knew that, but Walt Disney's value system was what? Family entertainment.

Now, did Walt Disney have a goal of making three times as much money? Absolutely, but the goal had to be attained without compromising his value system.

Once Walt Disney hired a group of efficiency experts to come in and analyze the Disney Empire. When it was finished, the analysts came into the meeting and said something like this: Walt, after all this money and months of work, we've got one suggestion for you. We can guarantee that if you use our suggestion, you'll double your net profits. And here's the suggestion, Walt. All you have to do is to introduce beer into the concession stands of Disneyland. You already have people there dispensing drinks, you have the cups, you'll just have to unplug the orange soda pop and plug the beer into it. You can get four bucks for a beer; you can only get one buck for a soda pop. No overhead increase, you should easily double your net profits.

Walt actually had nothing against drinking at all, but he ushered the analysts out of the room, saying on so many words: Thank you for your suggestion, I think it's a great idea, a major breakthrough. However, beer and my value system are not in line with each other. Therefore I can't accept your suggestion.

Some things have changed at the Disney empire since Walt's death, but that is the way it was while he was in charge. And so Walt Disney, who has been one of my mentors, is now on my virtual board of trustees. When I get ready to make a business decision, I run it by Walt. I say, "Walt, here's what I want to do." And Walt says, "Tell me your values again. Tell me your vision." And I do. And he smiles and turns his hands out, palms up, and says, "Well, then." And I know the answer.

I have my father on my board and a lot of people I've met over the years and some I haven't met. You get the idea. Who is going to be on *your* board of trustees?

I've asked this question of a lot of people. Recently I asked a junior in high school who was on her board of trustees. She told me she would have a certain young veterinarian she knew because she wanted to be a vet and because she found him to be skilled and understanding with the animals and also skilled with people. He got the facts when there was a disagreement or adverse reaction and let the attacks of emotional people roll off. For him such things are not personal. He's logical and rational, she said. I thought those observations were very wise. This young woman will be a lot happier if she can hear and believe that message—it's not personal—whenever she's having a hard time with people. And looking at the facts with logic instead of emotion is a valuable skill of powerful people.

When I looked at the third base coach, he turned his back on me.

BOB UECKER

This same high school student also named her mother to the board: Divorced when the schoolgirl was only five, the mother put her brother through college and her through a private school. "She supports everything I do. She says I'm her hero!" this young woman said. So when she needs to look at something very objectively, she calls in the vet to consult. When she needs support and confidence, she calls on her mother, either literally from the next room or figuratively in the enduring image she carries of her mother in her head.

Many people ask the question, "What would Jesus do?" And that helps them decide moral questions. How you work with your board of trustees varies. Do what works for you. In the face of attack, you can ask yourself what would Dr. Martin Luther King, Jr., do? React with steadfastness and nonviolence, I think he'd answer. What would Mother Teresa do? Give comfort.

Many heroes or powerful people who might be on your board are less than perfect. It's impossible to find a perfect person. That's okay. You don't worship these people; you use them as you would any other board. You use their strengths. You ask them about the areas where they excel and what they value. No one on your board is perfect, but they all have vision and power, and together they have all the characteristics of the extraordinary person you want to become.

Another thing you can ask your board of trustees to do is tell you your strengths.

Letitia asked a group she was coaching to form a board of trustees and to write down what these trustees would say if they were asked to recommend you for a job or fix you up with a date. She asked them not only to write down the strengths this board named but also to write them in the style or the voice of the trustee. The results were amazing. One wrote in the beautiful, complex language of the 19th century General Sherman; one wrote in the street talk of a rap star, another spoke in the passionate abstractions of Malcolm X. One used Thomas Jefferson's prose and principles. Another spoke in the voice of Meryl Streep, an actress unparalleled in skill and dignity, who keeps herself out of the tabloids and headlines of entertainment TV shows.

Just as many athletes, not always the greatest athletes, become coaches of other athletes and sports teams, so powerful people of all kinds coach so they can pass on the wisdom that made them great. They can pass on the power of words, the power of completeness, the power of risk-taking, and the power of commitment. Many of them coach through words on the field and off, often from public podiums and on TV; many are motivational speakers or have written books.

True coaching may manifest itself in quieter skills like listening deeply, accepting authentic expression with empathy, asking powerful questions and reflecting the answers back to the person being coached.

However you make your life extraordinary, coach others, pass your vision on so that it may grow in the world.

TO WIN AT LIFE'S GAME

- People who prove to be powerful are usually those who are willing to listen to good advice, able to effectively evaluate the input they receive and willing to let others draw forth a measure of excellence they wouldn't achieve by themselves.

- You don't necessarily have to have a coach on site. Your coach or several coaches can be role models, people who act like beacons to call forth the particular quality you need depending on your circumstances.

- Critical to achieving an extraordinary life is having the right values. Rather than a myriad of goals and outcomes, think in terms of accomplishing things that contribute to your core values. It works whether you're being coached or being a coach.

We are given one life,
and the decision is ours
whether to wait for circumstances
to make up our mind, or whether
to act, and in acting, to live.

GENERAL OMAR BRADLEY

CHAPTER TWELVE

Don't Wait One Day Longer!
Do It Now

Everything you do sends waves that reach beyond the borders
of your flesh and mind. Go ahead. Make waves.

O N A HIGH GYMNASIUM WALL AT ATLANTA GIRLS SCHOOL, A private prep school in Atlanta, these words are emblazoned over the playing courts:

Have you ever seen a hurricane in motion,
Followed her path,
Kept up with her speed,
Tracked her intensity?
If not . . .
Just watch me play.

Brittany Flood, a young woman in the class of 2007, wrote these words while traveling with her school basketball team, the Hurricanes. Others found her words inspiring, and they ended up on the wall. I'm told the quotation aptly describes how Brittany lives; she's an outstanding athlete, scholar and leader.

What team do you play for? Give it a name and write down how you will earn the name.

Put the stamp of your vision on the wall of your playing field, on your home and family, on your community, on your profession, on your Grand Central Station. Then play from that vision.

Widen your sphere of influence from where it is to the horizon. You know how a pebble thrown into a pool of water sends rings of ripples outward? You know how a smile pushes little wrinkles out on either side and then makes others smile, and their smiles spread? Everything you do sends waves that reach beyond the borders of your flesh and your mind. Go out today and make waves.

I don't wait for moods. You accomplish nothing if you do that. Your mind must know it has got to get down to work.

PEARL BUCK

Go out and get complete, confess to a misdeed, apologize and make it right with someone. Do something to affirm a child's confidence. Make another person's vision of himself change and grow to encompass his capabilities and more. Go out today and listen, really listen to someone tell you how he feels. Write a letter of gratitude to someone who affirmed your confidence and listened deeply to what you had to say. Take a risk today, step out of the box that surrounds your comfort zone to a new, progressive paradigm that will make the world better.

As I do at the end of each of my seminars, I'm asking you to do something, not someday but in the next 24 hours from this moment. So get out your pencil and write down—you can use the end papers of this book—today's date and what specifically you are going to do to fulfill the following five requests within the next 24 hours:

1. *I will do something to make a child's life better.*

2. *I will live with absolute integrity for the next 24 hours, living according to my values.*

3. *I will see the most important person in my life and tell him or her what he or she means to me.*

4. *I will establish a board of trustees to guide my life.*

5. *I will pass on this message of living an extraordinary life to another person, whatever part of the message resonated with me. I will pass it forward either face to face or through a copy of this book.*

Today lean the extra inch. Go the extra mile. Put forth the extra degree of effort to power a new life. Go into Grand Central Station sure of your destination and aware enough to change course when it better serves your vision. Go even though the outcome is not certain, committed to give it 100 percent for the rest of Your Extraordinary Life.

So, as my final gift to you in this book, let me share the oft-quoted poem by Stephen Spender, which celebrates those who live extraordinarily. He refers to men and women who fight selflessly for what they believe in, are willing to sacrifice, and whose souls are filled with passion and purpose. My wish is that his words would apply to you and to me.

I think continually of those who were truly great.
Who, from the womb, remembered the soul's history
Through corridors of light where the hours are suns
Endless and singing. Whose lovely ambition
Was that their lips, still touched with fire,
Should tell of the Spirit clothed from head to foot in song.
And who hoarded from the Spring branches
The desires falling across their bodies like blossoms.

What is precious is never to forget
The essential delight of the blood drawn from ageless springs
Breaking through rocks in worlds before our earth.
Never to deny its pleasure in the morning simple light
Nor its grave evening demand for love.
Never to allow gradually the traffic to smother
With noise and fog the flowering of the spirit.

Near the snow, near the sun, in the highest fields
See how these names are fêted by the waving grass
And by the streamers of white cloud
And whispers of wind in the listening sky.
The names of those who in their lives fought for life
Who wore at their hearts the fire's centre.
Born of the sun they traveled a short while towards the sun,
And left the vivid air signed with their honor.

—Stephen Spender

Five Extraordinary Values

Did you guess the five values that all extraordinary people, including the five profiled within these pages, have in common? Here they are in the order in which Dr. Riekeman highlights them during his lecture.

Vision

A **vision** is a description of yourself, your relationships or your enterprise as you desire each to be. In dictionary terms it is "a mental image produced by the imagination." It involves **seeing** the optimal future with enough detail to make it seem real, as though it were already accomplished. That's why visions, like goals, ought to be written down in vivid terms. Vision and values are often mentioned together because a great vision is always founded on noble values. Of course, realizing a vision takes on-going effort, and that effort is usually sustained by constantly reviewing the way you would **feel** if the vision were accomplished.

Commitment

One's degree of **commitment** is not so much measured by the intellect as it is fueled by the emotions. Commitment reflects expressions like "unstinting devotion," "unreserved enthusiasm," "unflagging zeal," and it is driven by an expanding sense of the rewards that such emotional involvement can bring; thus commitment is dependent on the perception of the freshness or newness about the thing pursued. Sooner or later, commitment almost always requires a willingness to risk what **is** for the sake of what **could be.** Few, if any, great accomplishments come without a commensurate measure of sacrifice.

Faith

Although definitions of **faith** often are presented in a religious context, the kind of faith discussed in **Make Your Life Extraordinary** involves confidence and trust in people and processes. If we have had a positive experience with a person, say, one who has proven loyal under test, then we have a measure of faith that he or she will continue to prove trustworthy. Faith, therefore, as we use it here, carries with it implications of loyalty, allegiance and a high standard of ethics. Faith is not credulity or blind acceptance; it is instead based on assurance that expectations will be fulfilled.

Excellence

The noun **excellence** draws from the verb **excel,** which brings to mind competition against others or perhaps against one's own earlier achievements. It carries with it the idea of not only achieving top quality but also of the desire for ongoing improvement. Such quality almost always involves attention to the less noticeable aspects of a pursuit because, as the saying goes, "the Devil is in the details." Ironically, although "excel" makes us think of a competitive arena, with spectators cheering us on, extraordinary people demonstrate excellence even when nobody is looking or likely to know what was involved.

Integrity

The word **integrity** was coined in the mid-15th century from the word integer or whole number, and carries with it the notion of wholeness or completeness whether applied to ethics or physical structure. It also is associated with being undivided, undiminished or unimpaired. In both human relationships and pursuit of vision, it includes such ethical aspects as honesty, reliability and, in fact, consistency with a stated ethical code. Integrity of a relationship between two people, for example, begins with a clear statement of mutual expectations and an explicit or implicit agreement to fulfill those expectations.